LOLA
THE
INTERPRETER

ALSO BY LYN HEJINIAN

The Proposition: Uncollected Early Poems 1963–1983 (Edinburgh University Press, 2024)
Fall Creek (Litmus Press, 2024)
Allegorical Moments: Call to the Everyday (Wesleyan University Press, 2024)
Tribunal (Omnidawn, 2019)
Positions of the Sun (Belladonna Books, 2019)
The Unfollowing (Omnidawn Books, 2016)
My Life and *My Life in the Nineties* (Burning Deck, 1980; Shark Books, 2003; Sun & Moon, 1987; Wesleyan University Press, 2013)
The Book of a Thousand Eyes (Omnidawn, 2012)
The Wide Road (with Carla Harryman; Litmus Press, 2010)
Saga / Circus (Omnidawn, 2008)
Situations, Sings (with Jack Collom; Adventures in Poetry, 2008)
Lola (Belladonna, 2005)
The Lake (with Emilie Clark; Granary Books, 2004)
The Fatalist (Omnidawn, 2003)
On Laughter: A Melodrama (with Jack Collom; Baksun Books, 2003)
Slowly (Tuumba Press, 2002)
A Border Comedy (Granary Books, 2001)
The Beginner (Spectacular Books, 2000; Tuumba Press, 2002)
The Language of Inquiry (University of California Press, 2000)
Happily (Post-Apollo Press, 2000)
Chartings (with Ray Di Palma; Chax Press, 2000)
Sunflower (The Figures, 2000)
Sight (with Leslie Scalapino; Edge Books, 1999)
The Traveler and the Hill and the Hill (with Emilie Clark; Granary Books, 1998)
Wicker (with Jack Collom; Rodent Press, 1996)
The Little Book of a Thousand Eyes (Smoke-Proof Press, 1996)

Guide, Grammar, Watch, and The Thirty Nights (Folio, 1996)
Two Stein Talks (Weaselsleeves Press, 1995)
Xenia, poems by Arkadii Dragomoshchenko (translated from Russian with Elena Balashova; Sun & Moon Press, 1994)
The Cold of Poetry (Sun & Moon Press, 1994)
The Cell (Sun & Moon Press, 1992)
The Hunt (Zasterle Press, 1991)
Oxota: A Short Russian Novel (The Figures, 1991; Wesleyan University Press, 2019)
Leningrad (with Michael Davidson, Ron Silliman, and Barrett Watten; Mercury House, 1991)
Description, poems by Arkadii Dragomoshchenko (translated from Russian with Elena Balashova; Sun & Moon Press, 1990)
Individuals (with Kit Robinson; Chax Press, 1988)
The Guard (Tuumba Press, 1984)
Redo (Salt-Works Press, 1984)
Gesualdo (Tuumba Press, 1978)
Writing is an Aid to Memory (The Figures, 1978; Sun & Moon, 1996)
A Mask of Motion (Burning Deck, 1977)
A Thought is the Bride of What Thinking (Tuumba Press, 1976)

Edited Volumes

Poetics Journal Digital Archive (with Barrett Watten; e-book, Wesleyan University Press, 2015)
A Guide to "Poetics Journal": Writing in the Expanded Field, 1982–98 (with Barrett Watten; Wesleyan University Press, 2013)
Ghosting Atoms: Poems and Reflections Sixty Years After the Bomb (with Olivia Friedman; Consortium for the Arts and University of California Regents, 2005)
Best American Poetry 2004 (Scribner's, 2005)

WESLEYAN POETRY

LYN HEJINIAN

THE INTERPRETER LOLA

Wesleyan University Press *Middletown, Connecticut*

Wesleyan University Press
Middletown CT 06459
www.wesleyan.edu/wespress

Manufactured in the United States of America
Designed and composed in Arno Pro by Mindy Basinger Hill

"One" was first published in *e-flux journal* 134 (March 2023).
"Five" was first published in *Washington Square Review* 51 (Spring 2024).

Library of Congress Cataloging-in-Publication Data
available at https://catalog.loc.gov/
cloth ISBN 978-0-8195-0178-3
paper ISBN 978-0-8195-0197-4
ebook ISBN 978-0-8195-0198-1

5 4 3 2 1

For Larry

through the HOY

LOLA THE INTERPRETER

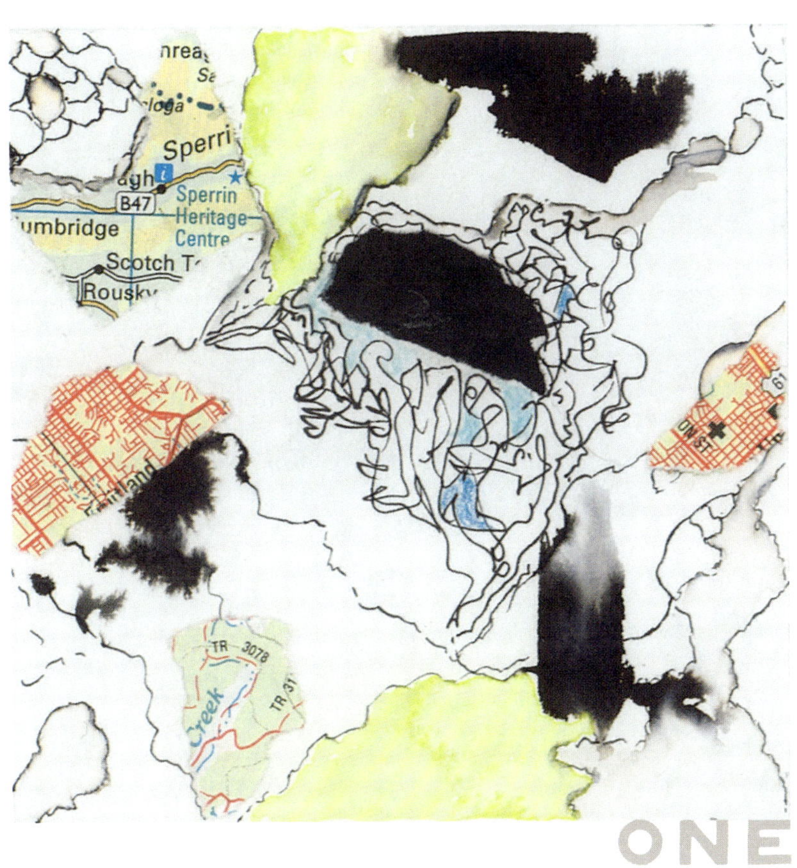

ONE

Shut up! Favete linguis! This is about to begin!

ADAPTED FROM HORACE

LET THIS BEGIN, precipitously disturbed. There: its only alternative now is to continue, which is to say: there's no real alternative at all. Skepticism—doubt: it can prove liberating: SKEPTICISM, says the motto, WILL KEEP YOU FREE. But it can lead to a sense of hopelessness, impossibility; it can seem to promise nothing but dead ends and fatigue: SKEPTICISM WILL EXHAUST YOU. Ergo, says the logician, freedom is exhausting.

With a change to my name would come a change to the things people want from me and a change of people wanting them, but needs and demands are not the product of a name, though it produces effects, they are, as it were, causeless, like the semi-invisibility (semi-transparency) of the Pleiades: explicable, therefore to some degree logical, though without cause. From across the small table Cyrus Ratad leans toward me: "Do you believe in freedom?" he asks. "That's a simple yes or no question!" he adds, jabbing his right forefinger in my direction. "Are you asking if I believe people live in freedom or if I believe they should?" "Simple yes or no question: Do you believe in freedom?" He is sitting taller in his chair—elevated by his ideology. "I'm not free now," I say, aware that I had agreed to meet him entirely out of a sense of obligation.

There it is: a fit of deviltry, then a fit of patience—or is it skepticism or disdain or a flash of irrelevant tranquility?

But fictions are the problem at hand: the fictions we are told, and especially the narratives we tell ourselves, limiting the possibility of human freedom. So let's consider human understanding rather than freedom. A play of words invites an act of understanding. Then reason outdoes itself. Understanding shrivels in the embrace of reason, atrophies in the cage of narratives' systems.

Say one bluntly states, "I've had a terrible day": Do we wonder who or what is to blame or do we cast the blame at the heels of fate as it runs ahead? One never sees fate's approach, only what remains after its departure. Happiness is never fashionable and always indescribable, but this can't be why we doubt happiness but never doubt unhappiness. Circumstances are conditional, everything is interconnected, we live in a medium of interpretation, etc. We know that a stone responds: the sunlight falls on it, it warms, its atoms vibrate more quickly, perhaps a tiny fissure opens somewhere on its surface. But we assume that it can't act of its own will; indeed, it cannot will, and therefore it isn't free. Facts are said to be true but not to be free.

Okay, but nonetheless I'll continue, "bargaining," as Lauren Berlant puts it, "with what is overwhelming about the present." In the kitchen, that theater of domestic life, a spoon eligible for a real superlative, a lettuce wilted through no fault of its own, worry of the kind that afflicts even infants, cream that the heat of the moment has curdled, a slow diminution of the shadows cast by a tree through the windows as storm clouds pass in front of the indifferent moon, gather. But I dream on, obviously, bound to the endless task of interpretation. In the dream, an overcoming man is like a female trucking elephant that's like a fallen pine tree to which he condescends or which he fells. The mind, lacking centripetal force, whirls and its thoughts are cast. Understanding is the mind's intended prey. Mind? I ask those who prefer to call it an absurdity. One puts a period at the end of the sentence. The sentence is identified by that mark as a stretch of significant time, a time that has fulfilled a purpose, however small, a time that has fulfilled an obligation (the thought has completed its sentence).

In "micro-pigment ink for waterproof and fade-proof fine lines," a sentence introduces Milly Margaret Willis, a retired child welfare attorney: "The place on her arm that Milly Margaret Willis accidentally smashed against a doorknob yesterday when moving a heavy chair hasn't recorded the event with a bruise." The sentence doesn't guarantee everlasting existence, and besides, Milly Margaret Willis is a mere literary character, she's not real. That's one thing that defies human understanding: nothing. Nothing prevented Milly Margaret Willis from banging the side of her right arm against a doorknob. There's a widespread belief that crossing one's legs, right over left or left over right, will bring some action to a halt. Perhaps this is why many men spread their legs when traveling, whether by horse, bus, train, car, or plane, or when talking. When conversation suddenly pauses some say an angel has just passed overhead but others say someone has crossed their legs—*they*, not *he* or *she*, because *they* is the pronoun of the unknown and that is something they have to admit, however much we may doubt its cogency. If there's to be skepticism, then there has to be a skeptical mode of subjective response to things in the world. This might assume the presence of a subject capable of, or susceptible to, skepticism, but if there is such a subject it would only be present at a moment and in one of its moods, while the cat it is sleeps or the shrub it is shrugs in the wind. This is the only present, the moment at which a combination is achieved, right here. Oops, gone! Hui!—another! Why would a poet, or indeed any writer, turn toward something close to fiction, you might ask, why invent characters, and one possible answer is that humans know nothing other than fiction, fictions are what thinking makes, fictions are the artifacts of synthesis, analysis, explanation, critique, interpretation. It's "where all could be justified and no one is just."

ON THE EIGHTH DAY of a calendar year I sit indoors reading with the cat on my lap. You could doubt the truth of that statement on multiple grounds, but let's stick to the overt untruth of it: I claim in the sentence to be reading but the sentence is written in the present tense, so I can't be reading: I'm writing. This problem can be remedied, and I'll fix it: I sat reading with the cat on my lap. There: I have cast it into the narrative past tense. I could continue; I could perhaps say (write) something about my sensations as the cat purrs (purred), or I might describe the street sounds audible through the open window (bus accelerating from the stop sign at the corner of the street as it crosses the intersection of Flats Ave and Rusty Street, heading south toward Oakland), or I could (though perhaps I shouldn't) acknowledge some source of anxiety or some object of inappropriate desire, I could draw the reader in with the narrative past tense as it begins to spread its fiction like fog over the present scene.

In one narrative, more historically credible than most, Lola poses a question and the question persists: Why does a poet insert characters into an essay? The answer is obvious: characters are everywhere, just look around. The *human* is a creature that cognition can't codify and understanding can't close. Though no field failure, here's the human goose worm hornet that nibbles the sky and lives as a rock in the forested sea. Or to put it otherwise, there's confusion. Interpretation then mobilizes diverse modes of arrangement. The character we know as Lola plays the stranger as she crosses a street so as to move away from the self-evident.

I first met Lola shortly after her birth, no more than two or three hours had passed, I had taken off my shoes. Nothing had yet begun, reality was as yet unpopulated, the cast of the world comedy had yet to arrive. "The natural result of any investigation is that the investigators either discover the object of search or deny that it is discoverable and confess it to be inapprehensible or persist in their search"—thus begins Sextus Empiricus's *Outlines of Pyrrhonism*. It's not inappropriate that the dates of a major propounder of classical skepticism are "uncertain": Wikipedia logs those of Sextus Empiricus this way: "ca. 160 – ca. 210 CE, dates uncertain." It is less uncertain, however, that he lived; though dying may undo the will to live, death can't undo living. I leave the date of Lola's birth unspecified—in effect, uncertain. Meanwhile, don't ask who I am.

It's in remembering my childhood and youth (but there's no remembering here, only storytelling) that I most forcefully encounter the impossibility of understanding my understanding, it disappears into the maw of infinite regress that devours being as it devours understanding. I'm not forgetting that individual being is as irrelevant as human expectation—human hope, worry, anticipation. The triviality of human concerns is pathetic—passionate. But, though irrelevance generates anxiety, frustration, and ennui, all of which make it almost impossible to continue, passion prompts us to begin. Mounting the bold carousel horse, awaiting the decision (which she is powerless to make) as to when it will set forth on its travels, does the child imagine a destination? The child can take the risk because she doesn't know what she's risking, she can enjoy the thrill of adventure and even of danger without feeling fear or fear of fear. The music begins—brass and drums, tuba, piccolo, accordion—and the horse heaves forward, there's no version of the story that doesn't have war somewhere in its far reaches or close proximity, distantly recent, the horse turns away and faces it: war is always in the wings. In the bas relief of vulnerability—the sculpting forth of being from the stagnant flat wet negativity of exposed clay—the vibrant hysteria of the artist (take, for example, the work of Julia Xanthe Lam) comes into view and is immobilized. The war horse bounds forward, charging in advance of the love plot circling the music in the middle of the field. But imagine the interpreter's shock to discover that the long affirmation she sustained in her childish enthusiasm couldn't nullify nullity, nonexistence, lack of being: the interpreter herself is a fiction. Some say that a human is a plant inhabited by a ghost, others that it's a stream of words on a course it can't gloss. Internal contradictions are everywhere; whether or not you find them intolerable is yet to be determined. Nonetheless, either really or not, here I sit, an occupant of an overcast chill damp silver January midmorning in a jumbled sequence of days glimpsing in the sky unidentifiable meandering details only peripherally perceptible whose drift I try to follow; it's like watching through a microscope the floaters in my eye. David Hume had it right: "Nothing is more free than the imagination of man; and though it cannot exceed that original stock of ideas, furnished by the internal and external senses, it has an unlimited power of mixing, compounding, separating, and dividing these ideas, in all the varieties of fiction and vision."

Every stone is a faceted fact, a 3-D quiddity, a thing. But a stone isn't a simple thing: for starters there's the gravity that holds it and the fire in which it was forged. It is gray and mottled green—like a frog and its setting shadow. Voilà: to see that one thing is not another is an extreme perception, producing an extreme experience. Cat and third grade teacher, jargon and compass, boeuf bourguignon and screwdriver, womanhood and surrealism—manifold differences in a fabric of associations. To set out to live the life you want to have led—that is the Nietzschean challenge—without a single detail changed, ready to live it again: stung by bees and stinging back. But all too swiftly we become habituated and blind to differences, or we become hostile to those things from which we differ; in either case, eventually a great continuity occurs, a dismal indifference.

The ancient Greek thinkers pondered over justice but thought little about freedom in our sense of it. Freedom in our sense of it? East of the city lie populated hills, under the city creeks are buried, between the hills are canyons, and rumor has it that each canyon harbors its own mountain lion, but at any given moment this is unlikely to be true. Things come into existence and depart from it "according to necessity," as Anaximander put it, paying "retribution" as they go "for their injustice according to the assessment of Time." Believing that the course of one's life was determined by the gods, the ancient Greeks could not value freedom; there was too little of it. Perhaps all that could be said is that to be free is to belong where one is, while the streets through the city are traveled by nomads. But things acquire their definition not on their own, autonomously, but from what's around them; they are given by their associations and held to them. Our sensations proliferate, fated to support another's panorama. But how can one characterize freedom as a condition of inseparability?

Zander Dallas declares one evening that for him the supreme value is reason. Why then is he a scholar of poetry? We are in a bar on a side street five blocks from the plaza where, moving three pretzel loops from a small bowl on the table between us, I ask him that question. "I believe in reason," he says, "but I don't believe in poetry." The pretzels are as pure as cactus. The former are the material made by mortals, the latter mortal material, but mere aesthetic playfulness no longer satisfies the old critic. Montaigne says that "philosophy is but sophisticated poetry"; in other words, poetry is the skeptic's philosophy. On the table lie seven daffodils, they are bound at the ankles—sold this way by the florist as if this were compatible with Western aesthetic values while reminding purchasers that prisoners, if they dance at all, dance in their heads. With this, comedy lies on the brink of death.

SO, WHAT OF IT?—I'm gaining the greatest pleasure from my current secretarial tasks: the invention of order and distribution of disordered thoughts and useless (dysfunctional) desires over topographical undulations, rivulets, back alleys, and storm drains where they can thunder and burble and romp and prompt compassion here and fury there; perhaps such tasks are proper grounds for a politics. Lola would object that the things that surge past or tumble by are just quickly and peremptorily thought-out whims, to which I'd retort: they are flapping from files and will pile into middens with architectural as well as columnar effect. Or I'd say they are barrels in a ring, a reference that makes her laugh since, at least for a moment, we acknowledge that while performing the role of a gadfly with the powers of an unmastered urchin, she is also a dauntless barrel racer. The fact is that Night has never yet unhorsed her. But let me return to my tasks, opening files to interpretation. Here's a wishful prediction that Camus recorded in October 1940: "This wind cannot last if each and every one of us calmly affirms that the wind smells bad." Let's imagine Camus in an apostrophizing mood as, with "Mediterranean fatalism," he poses a rhetorical question to the sky (or an outspread sheet of paper): O star, did you see the tide under the clouds? With such a sentence signaling a moment, calm is restored, then disturbed, and this, as Rosie Consuela Hassan would insist, justifies punctuation, or, at least, the comma. Written with a light hand, which is to say by applying a pen so that it makes only the gentlest of landings on a page, touching down only briefly and sporadically and hardly at all and with minimal to no calculation, commas appear, one after another just as stars appear as the night sky darkens.

With things I can see (like a pair of cowboy boots, a bicycle chained to a fence, a sprawl of nasturtium flowers, a plastic bowl, a child on a swing), as with things I cannot see (like time, suffering, knowledge, black holes, ennui), I'll play the phenomenal world's ongoing game of hide-and-seek. Carried forward by intuitions and curiosity, perception reaches the limits of logic and passes over them. *Fort/da*. We're just overhearing a toddler at play (they say it's Freud's grandson Ernst, who has a toy attached to a string), repeatedly discovering the principle of return—but how "innocent" is the pleasure of discovery? Say a human (some specific fastidious one—let's call it Monty Michael Leary) thinks about what's real in order to pull it, mold it, nurture it, pierce it, all the while assuming that every discernible phenomenon is unique and material, each manifestation just a scrap of launched particularized stuff. The conscious mind can have a strong impression of a blind window on a blank wall, or of an acidic sycamore on an urban street, or of a goldfish gasping in a glass of wine, or of a scrappy rat body scurrying, heaving, swaying through a city. Meanwhile, underlying consciousness lies the unconscious, lodged in the throat, perhaps, or pressing against the viscera or the genitals. So what is the mind, that something "appears" in it? And how very different from each other are water-borne insects, crepuscular rag rugs, and a fungus ring in a forest? What can a human understand, what empathies, what changes of mind or perspective can she or he or they or it embrace when surrounded by a reality imbued with what is unavailable—when, by being unavailable, things assert their alienation from human interests? Before I can deal with specious questions, a waking dream comes to me of weakness buoyed by Cheerios; I am reproached, and fall back, to participate in the widespread laxity that we interpret as getting along by going nowhere immediately or almost. A human such as Monty Michael Leary would say that to win a phenomenal game one must "invent interpretive strategies anew with every phenomenal form that one encounters." The winner then will be what Nietzsche in "On Truth and Lies in the Nonmoral Sense" calls "that master of deception, the intellect." If so, then so much for that great discontinuity Life.

As a teenager, Lola might have asked, if a tree falls, does it . . . etc., etc.—yes, of course, because there's never "no one," there's always something, with the fall of trees reverberating even in winter beside a creek rising under heavy rainfall. Every event has its own sound form, its own thought stack, its own noise construction. One can feel the full thrill of the event of the fall's irrelevance to the human world; it has dodged the prison house of human history. Coos from the pigeon fancier's yard continue in full compliance with the gleaming steel sky. Why remember anything—the resulting stories mean nothing, they are empty of everything but musty odors, old shit. What time is it, you ask; it's dissevered time, time split through the middle, time caught not quite on the dot but definitively on the line, half of now on one side and now's other half on the other through the long now we never quit. That—or rather *this*—can't be nullified.

Black sweater, black skirt, gray hair—I pass through Pug Blade Alley and, turning left onto Flagrant Street, I see a weave of shadows spread across an ochre façade. I am alive, part of the present, which is drawn out of the past: what in the past was in the future included me, making me also a presence, though not yet present, in the past. Or maybe not: as humans conceive of it, history (often occluded but also cruel, indifferent, destructive, stupid) doesn't provide a home for every moment. Yet history, in so far as *history* is a term for all that has happened (fate might be another), exceeds human historiography and includes not only all that is remembered but all that is memorable, which is to say everything (including the sound of the falling tree and the moss, twigs, redwood sorrel, and ferns onto which it fell). Roland Barthes (in *The Neutral*) speaks of "Michelet's ambition to give memory back to everything." Does this mean that everything that exists would be remembered or that everything that exists would be remembering? And on the basis of what, or, since we should narrow our options lest we drift into an infinite expanse of possibility as featureless as the void, on the basis of experience or of simple perception?

One would have to have absolutely no sense of humor to imagine that humans have ever produced a "simple idea." What John Locke meant by simple ideas were impressions or bits of information, passively received onto a tabula rasa, and thus made available for assimilation, combination, and development, but the tabula rasa hypothesis has been disproven. Perhaps what we begin with is indecision, grounded in its past, future, and the present's near synonym: eternity. We've no choice yet other than to imagine Lola as an unfinished person with wide distribution, or perhaps it's her rationality that's widely distributed, but, since it's buffeted by chance, the random, the trivial, the perpetual nagging of "the bitches of everyday life," its effects get scattered as if in obeyance to some airborne algebra, playground gossip, or mycelial calculus. Mistrust, thirst, reluctance, ambition: these are the spare parts of reason. Proliferation, speed, struggle, victory—in the right circumstances these are values, but so too are contemplation, generosity, strolling, indifference. Interpretation is merely a quest for a slower chaos. It departs from the center, it takes place in the margins and on the peripheries. So how do we explain? But why explain? It is always the same words telling the same lies. And yet having said that, I can hardly concentrate on a particular poem at hand, so powerfully does it thrill me with the strangeness and ubiquity of life. The thrill is in the living, without possibility of certainty, without possibility of universal assent. "The thought is obscure, the syntax gasps for air."

Let's consider the condition of the unlonely. There are times when the unlonely feel irritated at interruptions to (or intrusions into) their unloneliness, their solitude. Solitude is a sphere of one's own making, a sphere under one's control. There is an aesthetics of unloneliness for those who exercise their faculties with doubt and experience, but where would a politics fit into that? There is always something to address in public but it may not always be necessary to do so publicly, it could also be done indirectly or, better, obscurely, say by poetry, prophecy, or divination.

Rambling thought on shall walk ambling shock: this is minimal but not meaningless, a small materialized cluster of elements, a point (or surge) of conjuncture that forms a perceivable object rather than a cognizable fact. As it happens, I objectively like it, and, in a completely amoral way, I am the better for it. But I don't ask you to be better for it too, or wiser. Still, let's have more of it. At least for the moment we can change rhythm, change pace, pace again. Page again. *Thistle down loosens lock time while profligate hens drag duck straw.*

IF PUNCTUATION IS SCANTY (or absent altogether) we can assume that what's been written is poetry. The poet (some particularly interesting one) insists on developing linguistic syntax that can indicate the way in which the sentence is being used sufficiently on its own, without recourse to punctuation; to punctuate would be a form a cheating. But, you might point out, lack of punctuation can't for that reason be categorically poetic, since poetry is so often (and sometimes explicitly) engaged in cheating. And what we're calling cheating might in fact be an act of freedom, one that takes the form of liberality and munificence. Restrictions are lifted; anything is allowed.

For Aristotle (should we want to take him for our authority—and I don't see that we should) freedom is actualized by doing good and fulfilling one's obligations, neither of which are possible without a social context; to be free is to bind oneself to social responsibility, to happy sociality per se. At that I entertain a fantasy scenario of protestors during a pandemic: holding slender six-foot-long poles known as "social wands" in each hand, with which they measure the distance between each other, hundreds of students and workers are on strike in front of city hall, chanting, shouting, cheering. The contemporary social world, at least prior to the coronavirus pandemic and the "social distancing" everyone is told to practice, is one in which people are caught up in circuits of social negotiation, requiring circumspection and, often, some degree of dishonesty practiced behind a façade. One outcome of this is a sense of social alienation; another is complicity with common values that one, in fact, doesn't believe in. Those values cause certain kinds of behavior, shape that behavior, and, ultimately, bring about behavior's failure—and loss of freedom.

All the while, everyday life is underway, with trees, trout, bedbugs, humans, sand, crows, dogs, weeds, microbes, rocks, buildings, shrubs, glaciers, rain, and so forth living it. A long mottled dog on a narrow red leash tied to a silver bike rack beside a gray faux classical building plaintively watches me as if hoping I'm the human it's waiting for, but recognizing the dog I know who the expected human is and the dog whines. Sabrina Q. Wells, being consistently inconsistent, is predictable. She is animated, she veils strong opinions behind a pretense of confusion, she is snarky. Her friends call her "fiery"; others call her capricious or wacky. She now once again pretends not to see me, or does so until I approach the room she is exiting—then she vigorously strides out and slams the door shut. We should have outgrown this shit long ago. But contemporary (early twenty-first century) social relations may be dismantling bourgeois values (like collegial friendliness) right in front of us. We participate in, and our subjectivities as well as our public and private living spaces are shaped by, a constant social flow, which is, above all else, a narrative flow. Many of its narratives are false. We inhabit narrative communities; we both generate and receive narratives; we choose from among them and, having chosen, we set up camp within the story's bounds. Or we set up a tent in an Occupy zone in defiance of every story. The distinction between freedom *for* (choice, commitment, engagement) and freedom *from* (sheer freedom, mere freedom, the "abyss of freedom" of which Kierkegaard and, later, Sartre speak) is conceptually interesting but it may be only that and of little practical value. Freedom is a practice, ultimately, and as such, it exists in situ, in process, in uncertainty, and without definition.

For all practical purposes, one understands how things in the social world work. If x happens, y will follow. But if the name for x—the name by which we know it—changes, our understanding of the social world has to change, too; the social world, if named differently, would work differently. Day after day Philip Kilmartin sits curbside facing the door of the corner café, impassive, saying little and only when someone speaks to him, holding an empty paper cup, with a homemade hand-lettered cardboard sign behind him: "Need money for Rent by the 15th of the Month, Hungry, No Sugar." I am patient and pathetic, he thinks; I am persistent, but what's the necessity for understanding? "We don't know much about him," says Reggie Clara Toss, "except that he's here." She provides him with a chair from the café and, occasionally, a cup of coffee. All that's needed now are bits of information; when we have those we can slip shadows and story inside the outlines.

The imagination, disordered and murmuring or scrupulous and willful as it may be, by definition (qua imagination) either generates or receives images.

Aren't the eyes, too, instruments of imagination then, and the ears? As the sound of a "barking dog" reaches one's ears, isn't the "barking dog" an image, something imagined? And the dog itself?—some would say it's apparent, rather than real, but if that were the case, and if we were to characterize it therefore as a product of the imagination, it would have to be the product of either a collective imagination of vast dimensions or a concoction presented by whimsical gods or a 3-D quadruped mirage produced by some confluence of neurochemical and neuroelectrical forces. The barking dog would not, in any case, be sitting, trotting, or on watch along what Parmenides called (according to the evidence in the extant fragments) the "Path of Truth." And yet it was Parmenides who said, "It needs must be that what can be spoken and thought *is*; for it is possible for it to *be*, and it is not possible for what is *nothing* to be." Worrying about the difference (if there is one) between appearance and reality is too metaphysical; more lively and immediate is the difference (and there seems indeed to be one) between reason and irrationality. Lola interprets—or judges—art in practical, rational terms, and she finds it puzzling—entirely lacking in practical value, outside the realm of efficiency, too much bound to either immediate (temporary) pleasure or to materialism (the buying and selling of works of art), and irrational. "Okay," she says, "maybe it's rational to paint a landscape or a portrait of somebody, though doing either seems pretty useless." Lola is never insouciant but she is also never sullen when she spots a stupid thought. "Writing a love poem that impresses the person it's for could be useful, I suppose—or a poem that stirs up political feelings," says Lola. Still, from her perspective, it's all inefficient if not irrelevant. "Arggh—how can you take art so seriously?" I say I'll think about it and I raise my head and stare across the room at a wall hung with drawings, photographs, collages, small paintings above three bookcases set side by side and filled with books, their titles indiscernible from where I'm sitting but I know what they are and know the books contain thoughts and in some cases stories, stories and thoughts: ghosts, dogs, feminist theory, passions, accounts of entomological and anthropological research, plots, poems, theories of the good, literary history, the turn to language, commodity fetishism, art history, chaos. And all those thoughts and stories are exchanged and change from day to day or occur to humans as something entirely strange in their dreams.

Everything that exists is involved in perpetual processes of interpretation, simultaneously generating causes and effects. Perhaps an artist is a fantasy creature, author of a genuine inner life, but about whom, eventually, a police statement says that she or he died of weeping or, as some witnesses insist, of laughter. Moved by the pull and pulse of a long guitar solo audible through the speakers on the wall on either side of the bar and thus behaving little like the skeptic I claim to be, I flip my hand in time to a beat and protest, "Of course it's possible to have an idea and not know it." "The skull lit by eyelight," Samantha Jane Jenkins remarks. Thinking, almost by definition, entails receptivity; it's experiential. And each day is different from all others; chance takes its every advantage. "It was no longer the beginning that illumined and transfigured the everyday; it was the everyday that made the beginning intelligible, by supplying models for an understanding of how the world had been shaped and set in order."

EVERYDAY LIFE ASSUMES that lives are lived day by day, each quotidian life underway within a cultural sphere that's structured by habits, assumptions, beliefs, individual propensities, social and personal expectations, socio-economic structures and their requirements, material resources, and so forth. Which is to say that everyday life is underwritten to one extent or another by ideology.

And ideology can take on the aspect of fate. There it is: Belief, caught in the act of creating a fact. Will the fact make history? Or to rephrase that more capaciously, more variably, and more specifically: Will that fact *enter* history, will the fact *create* history, will the fact *fabricate* history, will the fact *alter* history? The link between fate (everything that happens) and time (naked as a rat's trailing tail) is obvious. How many everyday particulars—how much of the stuff and experiencing of everyday life—is experienced actively, consciously? People are conscious of things, but perhaps unconsciously conscious, as, for example, when negotiating a pathway around chairs and tables in a café or through pedestrians or traffic on an urban street. A pair of excited matched small dogs catches the attention of Jumi Brianna Stein, each excited dog secured by a yellow leash to a parking meter to the left of a man with his usual sign behind him: "Need Money for Rent by the End of the Month / Hungry / No Sugar." Jumi Brianna Stein automatically deduces that he has diabetes, steps into the café, greets me with a nod, takes her wallet from her bag and pulls a dollar bill out of it, steps back outside and drops the dollar into the man's paper cup, says "God bless you, too" to the man's response, and joins me at a corner table. The everyday is absurdly authentic! At a circular table nearby, a woman whoops with delight and applauds the vertical chocolate swirl atop the storybook pastry that Reggie Clara Toss sets in front of her on the circular table. Like most distractions, this one provokes an unwanted act of consciousness, and the unwanted act of consciousness provokes irritation, animosity, anger: a recontextualization of the moment, the place, the experience—a change in the situation.

David Hume states, "The command of the mind over itself is limited, as well as its command over the body." He goes on: "Our authority over our sentiments and passions is much weaker than that over our ideas." I don't disagree. I have little doubt that the brain crowns a system, though I don't believe that thinking must always obey it. The system crowned by the brain carries out a myriad of functions, but it doesn't construct narratives. The internet makes a clear (though perhaps suspect) distinction: "Brain is considered to be a physical thing, the mind is considered to be mental; the brain is composed of nerve cells and can be touched, whereas, the mind cannot be touched." But does the internet have that right? Don't we live by our senses in a tangible world, pushing thoughts aside, tossing ideas around, putting our mind to work on abstract problems or quotidian tasks? Metaphors—we cough metaphors, pant metaphors, sigh metaphors, and usually don't think about metaphors, but let's admit it: they're great stuff.

Thoughts wander; we should go in hot pursuit of them, unarmed of course: there's no utility, benefit, beauty, or intelligence in dead thoughts. That said, live thoughts are not always that great either, motoring us along without any sense of direction, until we chance on something of interest. Some experience takes place and we perceive it as an unassimilable whole, its temporality internal to itself rather than attuned to history, and then along comes art to poke a hole in it. The day loses its weapons, the small hole that a thumbtack makes in a wall comes to exemplify daily life. Consider the irreality of the hole: as the French say, "Into the shadows the hours go to hide."

TWO

To live is, in itself, a value judgment.
To breathe is to judge.
ALBERT CAMUS

MEMORIES CAN "EXPLODE" and scatter into different memories, catalyzing contiguous cells that form contemporaneous scenarios: a war-torn plaza is a placid park, what radar detects is reversed, a powerful judge drops her teeth into a flat lime-oil spritzer. New names are given—kind of unceremoniously, for sure: old rituals don't hold—so the named can embody stories *in concreto* and produce shocks (*vide*: as a flounder flies I scent undulating reeds!). The reconfigured stuff of the phenomenal world goes about its business in unfamiliar perceptual environments and a real-time *as effect* replaces the imaginary realm of *as if*. Take, for example, a man in my dream on a branch of a Douglas fir as he transmutes into a woman as a great horned owl in a dinghy. Intuition is enriched. And this is true even though we live in an endless process of continuous appearing, a continuum of experiences, breathing to bulk the air, dreaming pictures of fate. In and out we breathe scaled and feathered animate thoughts. Meanwhile, from some ground floor office on Flutter Street, the young data scientist is like "a 'subterranean man' at work," one who tunnels and mines and undermines; she is interpreting data about the city's underground infrastructure, buried roads, tracks, shells, bones, and the rest of the full subterranean realm through which its pipes, cables, and lines wander and into which its rods and pilings are thrust. Off she goes, down and around, chasing hairs, thumping hives, turning time: whatever were they thinking?

A storyteller is an agent of deception (especially of self-deception) and is it thanks to this that I maintain a sufficient sense of my subjectivity to feel assured that a continuity exists between what I perceived and understood in the produce aisle yesterday or while reading a detective novel or Aristophanes's *Frogs* (or whatever), on the one hand, and my understandings and perceptions today, on the other? And how does the thing itself that I perceive and understand sustain its "content" and "meaning" (significance, effects, reality) from day to day? I should get more exercise (this weekend I'll clean the refrigerator, scrub the oven, wash the kitchen floor), I think, as in another building Rosie Consuela Hassan asks a group of kids what the last two lines of Yeats's "Among School Children" mean to them. Rosie Consuela Hassan is suddenly aware that she's thinking not of what she's saying but of herself absurdly saying it to six rows of students in a warm room, thirty-three of them, all sixteen, seventeen, or eighteen years old and caught in the pathos, inanity, and hopelessness of "education" as it's repeated generation after generation to little avail. Everyday life is history, but history is dreaming (and Yeats is dreaming of history).

Meanwhile here is another sunlit two-faced February day floundering around like a spaniel in snow. A morning newscaster on NPR reports that "In many parts of the war zone, *people are going about their everyday lives* in the midst of the rubble" (emphasis mine). An hour later in the café on this overcast midmorning, Freya Cyprian Slight discovers a *tableau vivant*: having drawn four small café tables together, twelve women have gathered, each with her small baby, each baby curious, observing, one ecstatically paddling the air, just kicking a violet bootie off, one with clear drool on its chin, as the women, cooing and laughing as if attuned to ascending music, pass the babies between themselves, to the left, to the right, across the table, the tempo of the conversation unsettled by the rhythms of passage, the women tipsy from sharing infants, giddy from the milk in their babies and breasts. Doesn't studying literature ever strike you as ridiculous? Everything that's described, Freya continues, everything that happens, every character is imaginary. It's all fiction. To study literature is to study things that never happened.

Okay—as we encounter her, Mrs. Dalloway has survived the first World War and the Spanish flu, and on a sunny June morning in London in 1923, she is preparing to give a party—hardly the stuff of exciting novels . . . Except for when that crazy dude jumps out the window and gets impaled on the spikes of an iron fence (Lenny Ping Price waves down some attention)—gross! Standing in front of the restless eleventh graders, Rosie Consuela Hassan perches on the edge of her desk, demoting herself by assuming a casual—let's call it a collaboratively brainstorming—stance, though one might accuse her of subtly seizing a ledge of power. Was that an act of rebellion? And Mrs. Dalloway's party: even if its goal was to restore social familiarity, affective piquancy, and aesthetic surprise to everyday life in the aftermath of war and pandemic and even if it was able, at least for a moment, to secure social, if not individual, immortality, wasn't it ultimately an homage to passion?

Just as a fish emits melancholy bubbles [*breaker breaker!*], human reason troubles fate with questions. It clarifies thought with logic, but where does that leave wit? Humans would do better without provoking major events, without someone's making things happen. But, at least in the sociopolitical (though often also in the amatory) sphere, someone does make things happen just because someone else has already done so and the responding act might be remedial, or vengeful, or an act in a game of acquisition and power or in a mire of alienation. To Sylvie Win Sarrault, the three-year-old, trucks and ducks have a discovered relationship, a patent conceptual and linguistic connection—there's a system that pairs them, though the notion of systems has yet to occur to Sylvie in her Oshkosh pants, pink Crocs, and pale blue "Power to the Girls!" t-shirt. On the other hand, as the three-year old on her red and blue plastic "motor scooter" scans the scene, a neon-green truck turning onto the road and a male mallard duck landing on its grassy verge at the same moment are unrelated, purely coincidental and purely unalienated. Herodotus initiates the writing of history and even the concept of historicity itself as an account of interacting subjects, objects, and contexts, the prolix reciprocal presuppositions of matters and motion. In the end, though, every story breaks off way before it's complete. The site of interpretation is not a ruin but a dump.

Even if an *arrivant* waking out of context at the edge of a midland prairie I wallow there in self-criticism, it's how my narcissism asserts itself. The phrase "in a cruel country" has preceded me. Alone before the overcast sun, the day, like a scrap of fabric from the lining of a purse or an oilcloth liner from a pantry drawer or the breath of a cat or the sound of a mounted cop's shod horse on the street or the scent of diesel fuel and creosote along the waterfront railroad tracks or the feel of the scarred and carved slats of a painted wooden bench beside the path, has yet to make its call: how long it will be remains to be seen. One bequeaths by critique what applies to oneself as a living mind that is brought up short, and yet one can still *think* freedom. I reached the top of the trail past the landfill and turned back to look down and out, there lay the city, the bay, the nearer hills with stands of gray and tattered eucalyptus and somber live oak year round shedding their prickly leaves and somber reassurance, a scattering of California buckeye, too big for merriment and yet merry nonetheless, and bush lupine, and stretches of oat grass, foothill stipa, rye: description!

"I have constructed my case on nothing." We live in a warped topography of "foundational" narratives and transmitted interpretations, so let's compare ourselves to green balls or birds perched in a painting of hobnail boots, a russet book, and a sketchy wall, maybe a "boy wall." "[M]an must resolve to act, in order to exist." I'm quoting Camus again; this time he is speaking not for Max Stirner (as above) but for himself, not out of nihilism but out of absurdity; he is disalienating himself from others and from existence. Upward from a low C to a higher C, with both hands the pianist plays an octave and then ascends one note higher and then another, each note expanding the scale to make more room for the notes below. It's midmorning, we're far from midway between Icelandic laval life and the frantic human swirling that mills through the financial district in a storm while the glaciers fissure. Under shelter at the end of one long arm extending southwest, Lola negotiates a sharp turn and Night like a slung black hole speeds toward the finish line at the far end of the ring for practice.

IT'S NOT UNUSUAL FOR A CAT to jump onto a seated person's lap; it's not unusual for a cat to lounge there, so to speak, purring. Purring and producing effects: in this case, a sense of calming affective pleasure (what one might term *love*), which overrides a competing sense of displeasing difficulty (the cat has draped itself over my left arm) or momentary pain (the cat extends its claws against my lap) when I try to open my notebook and jot down some thoughts in response to what I have just been reading. We are back in the present tense of the second week of February: a pleasant warmth on my lap (the room is slightly chilly); a residue of orange and white cat hairs when the cat inexplicably jumps off my lap and walks away. But, as usual, we can't set aside the possibility that I am simply telling a lie, but inadvertently now. Let's grant my honesty but doubt, or at least question, my perceptions. And my judgment. And the grounds on which I base that judgment—general, though by no means specialized, familiarity with an animal commonly called a cat (at least in English). The phrase "commonly called" is important: we know the world (though we may not understand the world) largely by name. What if my perceptions were inaccurate, what if there were no cat, no city with its crushing concrete suppressing its muttering creeks? A boundary stone has been put in place—by whom and when needn't concern us at the moment; it sets the limit beyond which one cannot go. Some guy kicks the boundary stone—pushes against it—and rolls it farther along or rolls it away altogether. Wherever the boundary stone comes to a stop, it will set a new limit, for someone else who comes upon it; she, in time, will roll it farther. So it will go—each roll of the boundary stone reaffirms the mobility of limits. Hey—they have figured out a way to beat the fucking system!

There's an almost ethical character to what Husserl calls "a modification of belief," not toward what he calls the "neutrality-modification," which basically involves resting on an assumption (that manifestation of "neutral consciousness" characterized by "'merely thinking' what is performed without 'helping to bring it about'"), but, rather, toward skepticism and a transmutation of belief into a change of mind, a change of perspective, even an escape from (or at least a clear critical view of) commanding ideologies and their guard posts. Of course, one believes one's narratives because one wants systems and the stability and rationalizations they provide. Poems appear, composed in insubordinate iambs: celery iambs, axle iambs, and even political iambs—there's little in Lola's contemporary human milieu that hasn't been or won't be weaponized for political ends. Masks, beards, hats, schools, clocks, meat, cotton—they have all, at one point or another, been weaponized. Not so far from childhood, what does Lola overlook as she walks from home to work? As if they were people out for a walk on a city street during a pandemic, the pedestrians going about their barren business resemble zombies. They are both present and absent, as she with her fused parts feels she is with respect to herself, so far from childhood.

Famously Penelope weaves, perpetually bound to domestic labor. Artful at twilight and artless at dawn, she begins again. Such is her *Odyssey*. Sensation and sentiment are mediated by erotic thought swarming with conscious and unconscious contradictions. O peak and pit, you win! Penelope's shuttle flies, her scissors flail; Penelope is hot with anger, restless with yearning. Flinging aside the embittering monotony of unacclaiming unchimed time, Penelope pulls away, then she returns without a flaw. You say that reappearances are mortal, erased in a blink? From there abstraction is not far away, though it took painters many centuries to develop the logic that allowed it.

And now—that woman has no boundaries!

Inside the bank Cordelia Katrina Cabanatuan stands behind the bulletproof glass shield counting cash; timeless, says Jewassi Zhdanov Jones. Cordelia Katrina Cabanatuan either doesn't hear her or doesn't understand or doesn't care; Cordelia Katrina turns to the desktop electronic cash-counting machine and watches the bills flip through their recount; the sum holds its own. Wet ochres and siennas clog the curbside storm drains, an illegible short receipt from Safeway and a brown paper napkin from a take-out place are wedged into the trodden soggy sycamore leaves that have dropped from a street tree. Faculties of perception are said to be powers, but powers to what end and how often, if ever, are those powers not political in intent? Cordelia Katrina looks back at Jewassi Zhdanov Jones—but not over the left shoulder—or is it the right?—death lurks over one of them, or so she's been told: death, the entirety of the past (the world before she was born) and the future (the world as it will be without her).

The existence of time (if one can speak of its having existence—properly speaking, time, however complexly, is the *medium* for existence) precludes the possibility of total freedom. And therefore it precludes the possibility of any freedom at all, since freedom is either total or it doesn't exist. But why, one might ask, does time preclude freedom? History introduces discrepancies, and discrepancies provide the grounds for new interpretations producing new perspectives that assume different realities from those that precede discrepancies, whether they are acknowledged by a measuring scientist or a boastful parent. O Neanderthals, O Paleolithic cave dwellers, O Viking raiders, O Mongol hordes, O people preserved in peat bogs, the ballast that balanced your boats has been thrown overboard. It is to you that time pertains! I am King of Usage—I use, says Jonah Giacomo Martin, gesturing with his fork over a slice of pizza, and I, says Reggie Clara Toss waving her pencil and order pad, am Queen of Usage—I'm used. You can't equate passivity with mindlessness. And we are *so* over gender binaries!

There are many kinds of skeptics including those who, pulled one way and then another more by conscientious curiosity than dismissive doubt, remain perpetually inconsequential, and those who like Lola, young as she is, engineer their skepticism to speed through middling meadows like intelligence through the logic of conspiracy theories. But one way or another we all extend our bodies through space at different rates, plodding or dashing, tromping or scurrying, dallying or racing, and so forth—forth of necessity. Three strolling—or let's say ambling (indecisively? aimlessly? slowly, for sure!)—Mount Foot Avenue pedestrians occupy the do-it-yourself space that uncurious hurrying impatient pedestrians feel a right to rush through. And that story, "pure fiction," solely invented here as it is, is continuous with our own. I am just one of many irritable efficiency-demonstrating pedestrians pressing past as I mutter "Excuse me" in protest, righteous in my unironic sense of my importance. But too soon I'll get to a subsequent day, "a corner made of red mud." Or not: Everything I say is a lie, I say, and Lola shrugs as she smiles: You're shifting from skepticism to paradox—that's so totally pessimistic! Everything begins but from something. And something too began and continues to begin. Continuities are synchronous with beginnings—or one could say continuities are, well, continuous with beginnings. Tony van Heuvel gestures with the mic in his hand toward the ceramic cluster of forms on exhibit, Nowhere is the historical continuity of art absent, he says, so where do we see it here? No forms without precedents, Sammy Jane Jenkins says; I'm not thinking of Plato, Sammy adds. You're talking about material form—particularity—not ideals then? Behind Tony van Heuvel there's an open window but beyond it there's nothing to be seen, no reference points, no objects, no signs, it's blank but without even showing a blank; he might be backed by death.

SOMEWHERE WORDSWORTH REMARKS that Shakespeare could not have written an epic; he would have died of plethora of thought—this according to Francis Turner Palgrave in a footnote in *The Golden Treasury* to a sonnet by Shakespeare. Each thing (object, entity, event, situation, encounter, relationship, etc.) has an infinite number of possible ramifications, implications, purports, meanings, histories, mutations, futures, connections, etc., and extension in time and space: infinity is one of a thing's dimensions, plethora is one of extension's features. An allegorical statue said to represent abundance stands on top of a museum overshadowed by the towers of the financial distract. Okay: live and interpret. Once we have those two, there's overlap. We may get Venn overlap, or deposits and sediments and palimpsests, or braidings and intertwinings, or matings and the production of third things and thirty billion. Before the corporate and capitalist towers appeared, the sun fell on abundance. That's one way to put it. Another might be: abundance rose to the sun (like a rooster).

Often the reasoning human is like a squirrel or packrat putting things in strange or unwarranted or unreceptive places. This so-called reasoning human will speak to an object, say a charm bracelet, eggbeater, poppy, cell phone, duck egg, pencil, rake, baguette, fire engine, toothbrush, jackhammer, cow, two-tone racing bicycle, serrated bread knife, plastic buddha, or tattered copy of *The Sibley Field Guide to Birds of Western North America*. Or something else. You name it—or, better, speak to it. I'll leave the resulting scenario to you; every occasion is particular and unique. What will you—what might any reasoning human—say? Hola, piano; whassup, omelet; yo, sunflower? We live in a general absurdity, some of it happily genial, some of it annoying or worse, but it couldn't be otherwise: absurdity bobs, burbles, splashes, and cascades along many branches, tributaries, and into and along creeks, rivers, brooks into swimming holes, pools, estuaries, lakes, marshlands, bayous, and the sea. Meanwhile, markets have to be created, and then they have to be set free which is to say given over for common sense to assume as naturally (demonically) as an infant nuzzles a breast. It could be said that there is little difference between a dead wall and a cliché, but an overly familiar "truth" is more easily penetrated than brick or bars—and yet those familiar truths take years of homework and classroom drills and subjugation to bullying to get established in a human mind, while walls are only exterior. So Sabrina Q. Wells improves her posture and diets, she stands taller and loses weight, she lengthens and thins, she adjusts her narrative, tweaks her story, is insistent, reframed. Sabrina Q. Wells sells her RAV4 and gets a helmet and a Vespa. With too weak a sense of humor and too strong a gift for pomp, Sabrina Q. Wells takes to calling her Vespa "the real": I'm going out for a whirl in the real, she says, amusing only herself. As relatively often, here Louis Aragon has it right: "There are strange flowers of reason to match each error of the senses."

Christa Wolf speaks of one's becoming "irretrievably lost, because enslaved to one's own, deep-down consent." In Wolf's account, the circumstances to which that consent was given belonged to the mid- to late 1930s in Germany; she's referring to the Nazification of life, sudden but with its effects immediately becoming second nature. And now? Something might be returned from the void we call memory, the maelstrom of false contexts that nonetheless can familiarize us with them, bestow them with identity and caption them as if with a title printed on a label attached to a wall beside a painting, something like *South Stolen Street* or *Plutocracy Gardens*. But for now we have to think a free radical present, though it's *highly reactive* and *has a short lifetime*.

Looking down on two cars and a delivery truck from my window in this idiosyncratic February storm, I watch their windshield wipers swinging back and forth as if over a protective screen of time. "A protective screen of time"—meaning what, that the screen is obscuring time or that it is time itself at the work of obscuring perceptions? Attention offers its invitation to time but it always just misses the present, even as the present allows the future to become the past. A certain Lorne Falkenstein (a scholar of eighteenth-century philosophy), in an essay on David Hume's understanding of "temporal experience," remarks, "Phenomenologically, as musicians speak of themselves marking (not making) time by playing music, so the parts of time are marked (not made) by the coming to be and passing away of perceptions, with the present moment being marked whenever an impression comes to be or passes away." Even if every living thing, both as cause and effect, participates in conscious metempsychosis, fully remembering its past lives (and maybe those to come), sameness wouldn't occur. Coming back as a human is not like being the garden salamander it was before nor the hummingbird it was before that. Sufficiently enclosed to prevent a full experience of time and thus imprisoned within too much similarity, instead the human will wildly dream different things into view; they would appear: a dancing door, a box-rock-bun-bear, an androgynous earthquake on stilts, a horse of clear water, and other unlikely things, all gathering around a camp storm on a vertical beach.

For what seems a long time, the eyes of the cat don't stray. Why then make a distinction between the unseemly world awake and the unlikely world in dreams? Indifference has no concentrating surface, that's the province of contexts, determinations. Suddenly the cat digs in and vaults into the world of experience, recipient of a signaling composition, a panoply of enhancements, a bevy of converging details, a host of promising implications, and a few scraps of impersonal threat. We may say that probability demands, we may say that chance nullifies probability, we may say that the transmutation of a russet brahma steer into a wolf prowling in its summer coat is not just improbable but impossible, we may say that existence is not made to order and that it can't organize: how sentimental we are! Neither the knocks of history nor chalky fictions and certainly no dreams or drawings or perpendicular individuals on bicycles or dappled gray horses are representative and they don't teach "universals." We may be surprised as things move in and out of selfish solitude. But Lola bears no messages; Lola and all mean to be here, that's all. And a point has been made, "[W]hen we see something, we must think something in order to see anything," but it's only a point.

Lola in the always fragile present tense sits, limbs tense, legs crossed, inattentive until she notices irregular beats of humans in the distance, carpenters with wood, two bankers playing ping pong in the neighbor's garage, a tall youth dribbling a ball as he comes up the street, a woman in high-heel boots descending a flight of metal stairs. Too judgmental, too demanding, that's Lola, but always playful, says Noor Bigelow. There's unease under the bed, along Upper Alley, in the map room of the Department of City Planning and the Environment. Concurrent with the labor of representation, the labor of secrecy proceeds, the work of keeping secrets. As in Homer's story, where Penelope's furious shuttle makes its shots and trembling fingers withdraw the resulting lines, daily life continues: repetition is intrinsic to domestic labor's erotic game.

What changes is always something. We can't cut a thing from its contexts in our perceptions. A thing arrives (appears) in an assemblage (constellation) of things whose corresponding appearance informs its context, and each thing arrives with a history and prior contexts—its *determinations*. Determinations are mutually reciprocated and presupposed; people and places are among mine, also of Lola's, and those of Reggie Clara Toss, Ben "Blister" Baxter (whom none of us even know), Loretta Jon Minder, etc. And having said this, we can now appropriately (as cast, emboldened characters) use the pronoun *we*. We should all meet death, Loretta Jon Minder says in an email to Zander Dallas, with vitality the way the tabla with an expectant echo meets the sitar in a raga. Nothing can be precluded, neither walls nor pilot lights nor books nor chocolate mousse nor delusions nor carbons nor palominos nor tugboats nor feminisms nor sleeping pills nor weeds nor air-conditioners nor passions nor their contexts in our feelings.

IT'S LATE FEBRUARY and already that is a fiction: it's the last week of a false February then, but February is often false, a chaos *en passage* as false as the promise of freedom. She is a fatalist they say of Jumi Brianna Stein. Hilarity is everywhere and abundant. Dressed in ripped jeans and wearing candy-blue shoes, she walks up Higher Avenue in character, branded and labeled and going past trees that are living their own less disclosed and more gradual lives, or so it seems to Jumi Brianna Stein, as if this were an interpretation providing a new truth to claim. There's not much difference between them, after all, interpretation and interpreted are each perpetually claiming. Having vividly posited herself to the world, Jumi Brianna Stein has deranged indigo, and with that the world now vividly posits itself to her. There stuff can take the form of colored marbles to be set like clenched teeth in a glass bowl serving as the centerpiece on a blood-oak dinner table. Or it can appear as handfuls of sand, mycelia of allusion, pebbles tossed high into the air above a creek. Of course, all of this is a fiction as I am and (more obviously) Freya, Jumi Brianna Stein, and all the others named or unnamed here, all the dramatis personae (see "Afterword"), the recipients and/or purveyors of (continuing and/or fragmented and/or contradictory and/or engrossing and/or marginal and/or banal and/or recurring) story lines that are never straight and interpretations that are never verifiable casting nodules into "the rebarbative spectacle of atoms jostling each other in the void."

In *Great Expectations,* Dickens's great novel about the *fait accompli,* the future hovers, the past lies in abeyance. So why our obsession with the weather? The real trudges along inside history from which we can read grand systems out. Okay, so the wheel wobbles; it's reinvented—what did you expect, when what you want are new grammars giving new places to go? We need more words for moods; back when Milly was in school *stress* and *panic attack* were terminologically unknown and therefore not experienced. So what about *rugged* for the feeling of being besieged by demands from every direction and *stapled* for having a sucky job. Cyrus Ratad is now in the wide worried stage of comedy, but of course, people are always in the way and thus envy and petulance and gossip can unfold and song. Comedy is the high art of low life and the low art of high life, all named for their effects on the innards. And the weather, like the ancient gods, is impervious to our prayers, indifferent to our concerns and undisturbed by its own effects.

There's no uncluttered day, no taking of siestas, no honor among plutocrats, autocrats, or kleptocrats, no clearing away of soil-crushing concrete, no silence unbroken by shouts, honking, and machines, no songbirds singing at dawn, inside or out. Then try this—it's multiple choice (Cyrus Ratad has his hands palm down, slender fingers outspread on the café table): Which would you prefer, to be part of the action or away from it and at peace? Inside or outside? Every phrase, line, sentence, stanza, or paragraph, not to mention each mumble, proclamation, command, question, statement, whisper, request, declaration, or scream, is trying to make its escape from some epistemological genre. There you have it: comedy sparks camaraderie; tragedy sends us separate ways. Just as a street musician plays his accordion with a light brown open shoe box set eighteen inches from his feet, so an aspiring epistemologist might take up a study of conscious contextualization ("Want to know whether your friend's crazy ideas come from observation or inspiration?—then you are a budding epistemologist!") or what they call *orientational understanding.* But tragedy can't turn people into detectives.

In the most recent film adaptation of *Great Expectations,* two detectives (giving the *dramatis personae* an update) are (as required by the genre) in conversation as they drive (at night past a pawnshop, a liquor store, dark buildings on a wet street) to the scene of a crime (nature unknown) and one of them (could be Placo Paris Wang, could be Materia Tamayo-Cole) brings up the idea of "historical form" (downdated metaphysics); the topic drops as they arrive. Realism is quotidian and therefore full of holes, an observation that leads us into metaphysics; the thorough detective discovers a void in quotidian places and identifies it: fate. Holes happen—that's the reality for which realism should be held to account. In the plot there's an inexplicable gap, an abyss without cause, but obliteration doesn't necessarily follow. A detective's job is to find a cause and come up with its explanation. She begins with questions tinted by metaphysics: What are first justifications? What's original cause? What lays out the course that crime runs? Iconography can get transposed from one system to another, standing figures can be read as amiable or hostile, akin to us or strange, inspirational or as horrifyingly objectionable as the face that, in a nightmare, appears suddenly at the window leering at us lecherously and hungrily, not *like* but *as* a carnivore. A week later, everything may be exposed. People live ideas just as much as they live lives. While a poem commits linguistic acts of aggression, its line breaks short-circuiting certainty, its phrases taunting perception, we can believe in the credibility of prose and the possibility of fiction. There's nothing universal anywhere here, all that the logic at work in this (wherever there *is* logic) can arrive at are particulars—nodal singularities. But we can say on their behalf that they may serve as catalysts to concepts and points around which events and their particulars can cluster and accrue. Thinking, with its perpetual inner contradictions, is a *perpetuum mobile,* angling, with "a strong taste for ambivalence and contradiction" and "a sense of irreducible complexity," into cosmoses (or, more felicitously as well as more correctly, cosmoi). But I will leave it to you to visualize this.

Tamarind Magee in a navy false-turtleneck sweater, Zandar Dallas putting his dark glasses back on as he leaves the bank, Pilar with one hand holding the brim of a large black sunhat on her head, Aquo Thomas Koury carrying two take-out coffees as he steps to the left around two strolling women, Reggie Clara Toss pausing under a shop awning to read a cellphone text: bringing things and names into conjunction, the interpreter presents sheer adjacency as a site of meaningful interconnectivity and interpurposiveness. As for me: I can't pretend to be familiar with the world, the enigmatic other; I just participate in the comedy of interpretation. But with some seventh sense, I notice the shift of the place of things, know (sort of) stuff in its own drift, my picture of the world drawn inside an impudent frame. And behold, just as a log gives a river an inducement to err, so a fallen electric scooter stalls a dog, its leash caught on the handlebars, and jerks Freya Cyprian Slight, "the young data scientist," to a halt just as, arms out, she's leaning eagerly forward to embrace her boyfriend Fiasco Bikash McBee, "the disillusioned techy." Fiasco will never be a tech bro—they all suspect annihilation and assume different personalities, having none of their own to maintain, or so he thinks. They change but trivially and incompletely: there's no metamorphosis, there's no future. There's no comfort in the realization that at bottom human nature hasn't changed since "cave man" times despite prisons hay bales bathtubs swallows minivans live-work spaces schizophrenia cellphone towers English muffins bunions dictionaries troglodytes reams of paper raptors microbreweries wars. But all of those are necessary: history has its translation machine, which is memory, and it is always in need of nudging and new parts. And here we might undertake a study of the anatomy of a cauliflower.

Perhaps everyone lives amidst widely distributed distractions that discipline one into distracted states of mind. The wood chipper hitched to the back of the city's white pickup truck roars as the tree trimmers feed tossing branches into it, producing a form of artificial lighting, severed from material structure, sonic in origin. Helicopters lift off, abandoning refugees on a rooftop. Nine time zones away rising flood waters sweep away a cop in a car. The unseasonably warm late February weekend is all a theater piece, its furniture arranged politically but with no feel for its utility, table with its legs reaching for the sky, humans on their sides merrily rolling down grassy hillsides, pigeons mooing mournfully.

What is that foreign language that I can't speak and that threads somewhere through an interior imperceptible behind ideas that the mind generates with contradictions weaving and colliding through them and obscuring things impossible to know? It sits, that language, shaking with logic, but the rules and reasonings that its logic follows belong to an alien semantic landscape. It rules the individual, what Fred Moten calls "that brutal, brittle crystallization of an always and necessarily incomplete melding of subject and object." But let's keep things suggestive, not conclusive: yes, it's a skull, but look, it still has some hair. For real aesthetic experience we should try terror, something triumphantly shown of everything churning up from the faceless deep glass of the sea. But as you can see, I'm neither lost in the depths of perspective nor detained, at least not for long, by the impeding power with which grammar can imprison words or the unknown nullify the validity of the perceptible. Scattered through the present there are instructions for continuing onward. And for one thing, we have to avoid attributing universals to particulars. When Flaubert, in his oft quoted letter to Louise Colet, tells her that he wants to write "a novel about nothing" (with *Madame Bovary* being the ostensible result), couldn't one posit that the *nothing* in question is, in fact, the murkily quotidian *everything*? Subject, object, and abyss: the stuff of syllogisms? Stories depend on the if-effect. Without it what can Lucy, Polly, Nora, Rosie, Sam, Jane, and all the rest do? Well, they are gone, and here must I remain. One of Rosie Consuela Hassan's students promises that she's going to dig into "This Lime-tree Bower My Prison" for deeper meanings and Rosie predicts in return that she'll produce a paper of holes.

verdi, a progen
que style that Bach
pogee. First up is
nta Vergine," a liturgic
us and orchestra that
ith its large-s
BREME
NABRÜCK

THREE

March a one march at once march
at one march for once.
GERTRUDE STEIN

WE MAKE THE BEST and the worst use of time by relegating it to postponement, deferral, waste, irrelevance; we send it out and away from things that can be thought or done; we estrange time from reality and thus from life's activities; and in the process we either liberate ourselves or find ourselves stranded, and it's probably the latter.

Just as baboons, ill-at-ease and querulous as the sun sets, move about restlessly and shout to no effect, so humans in March, the twilight of winter, grow irritable, anxious, and uncomfortable as the long familiar routines of everyday life deplete rather than sustain interest, energy, and appetite. Reality, lacking energy, begins to lose credibility; the past, running out of reality, begins to lose possibility. Lola quickly laughs sardonically when she spots the title of a book on display in the window of the bookshop on Higher Ave.: *March: A Comprehensive History of Humanity. Universality for Idiots,* she thinks. Unity—coherence congealing into a whole—is illusory. Tony van Heuvel, nonetheless, refusing to blink a way out of a state of willed self-deception, gazes out a window into the midground of trees blown by the wind as if expecting to see the perpetual play of time with truth though there's nothing but mist to be seen between the boughs. With what goals do we engage in introspection? There's always the grand plenitude to come, the promised comedy when everything comes out, but this is just another labyrinthine day in the life, etc., with fence fibers half buried in rain. The past of *the man of the hour* recedes by the minute, the past of *queen for a day* has lost relevance. Her past is only a receding dim version of the woman who repeatedly steps slightly away from the life she has led, leaving dull fragments of it behind. What we have is a sequence of parts that can be unified only (mis)conceptually by an imagination bent only on eliminating details, the devilish essentials that are the *sine qua non* of reality. It's only with a pencil drawn over a rough ridged surface that the illusory continuities on which a coherent imaginable life is predicated can be seen. Continuities are lost, only commas remain where long sentences and full paragraphs used to fill some time across some space. Penelope moves among her suitors or Penelope sits by day and again by night at her loom, she is either performing domestic labor or, as one fifth-century BCE Greek philosopher proposed, she projects "an image of the faithful labours of the philosophers."

A woman is awake, she can't sleep, no need to know why, she's restless, wagging, maybe imagining herself giving a speech, speaking out, no need to know the cause or content, it may not be the reason she's awake, wagging, restless, raging, maybe she woke just to reprimand the night, to whip the horses of the night, never to repeat. Humans may always have similarly hated, raged, enjoyed, marveled, worried, disdained, feared, and loved, not to mention shivered, sweated, danced, wept, sat, pissed, swallowed, laughed, slept, and fucked—we are unbeautiful beasts all of a kind—but given the vast amount that the things that repeatedly press on human thought haven't changed, isn't it likely that over time thinking minds have stayed the same? Some ants drown in a toe-deep creek and it's because of just such incidents that Democritus "developed a thorough critique of the trustworthiness of the senses." Though we make use of our different senses to coordinate our resulting sensations so as to figure out and focus on what's present, what's going on, we can't similarly coordinate our emotions, our moods. And where anaphora doesn't naturally occur, we invent it. Wakened by a siren at an early morning hour, I look out the window at two red emergency trucks and, with their flashlight beams playing over the side of the house, five fire fighters in black invested with the right to look back at *me*. Neither ambivalence nor doubt nor uncertainty nor skepticism will secure us any immunity from that. Night: that is the name of the horse that over and over

Lola imagines riding through long insomniac hours. Raccoons emerge from a drain pipe into the dark, chortling, giggling.

The quiet light of a returning normal life is interrupted by the roar of nomadic motorcycles—seven—plunging out of Chance Alley, it's an unexpected event without perceptible inception, it's suddenly appearing on (or being spontaneously released onto) Flutter Street, where a chancy I, never fully objectified, pulls back. Nothing: nothing though twice yesterday I found myself consciously noticing and noting something, as if in preparation for remembering it. Both times, too, I immediately felt that such noticing was a form of cheating, of forcing memory rather than simply being open to it. Say you are a character encountering a story. Stop the story. Got born. Get a name. The name won't fit but you'll have to wear it or go through the hassles—bureaucratic and social—of changing it. So many hassles! Too many homilies! And remember: these aren't characters but names and names need to be differentiated from both the named and from personifications. Take my word for it: there are no allegories here. Our particular interpreter is looking for ideas to hold provisionally; they'll be evasive, she's a subject after vacillation, incoherence, doubt. Where there might be a name, there's pathos.

Everyday life requires at least a modicum of agency. We gather things that make an appearance, we embellish the quotidian with a sequence of vivid social moments. A young friend tells me the saga of an unfolding multi-mishap housing crisis that continued over the course of the entire first year of her postdoctoral fellowship at a small distinguished bastion of established white life, where the crisis took occupancy of her psyche. Next a young woman, frequently touching her face, frequently pulling both sides of her hair across her cheeks, "shares" confidential information, which is okay, it's hers to confide, I can only listen. Somewhere lurk the principles of selection determining what I hear, what I remember, elsewhere lurk my principles of description, my principles of narration.

In the (loose and close) grip of ambivalence, we are both deep inside the zone of choice and on the fringes of the conditions and circumstances that demand one. We are often striving to become what we are not, or is it playing that we are doing (play-acting, costume-displaying, lying, wielding ourselves metaphorically) as we struggle not for an ideal but for an alternative? Becoming personable, baby Deli looks up, giggles, wriggles, looks down, and intently squeezes peas, seizing or selecting, three or four in each plump ardent hand. Georgina Gerald Brown is responding—enthusiasm being a social value—to what's neither false nor true. Here on a key is a haptic fingertip, a cognitive partner in the machinations of the mind, it's tucked under the nail of an indexical finger that partners likewise with cognition but to different effects. This is a signifier, that the signified—and over there is an observer, a spectator, whose presence has to be ignored. Nearby a person on a "wrong track" passes, erring autonomously; there is no accompanying verse. Think of all the imprecisions (and ambitions) of the language of naming, the language used by those in thrall to eternal strivings and the quest for perpetual self-improvement! An aporia can't be isolated, it's not a sticking point but an extension into the temporal interior of an interminable through-zone. Every performance (and all performativity) is tantamount to transition: *mended when what grass lift is* and *slippage slat bough in metal drift if.* A falcon is nesting on a parapet overlooking a dream city in a dream not of a falcon but a dream of slow flight, a dream slowly reached—a dream flown to without city sounds, without shouts, without the acceleration of a car on an adjacent street, a train whistle from the distance, a train to another dream or from one. But this is prose, not dream. There is that third acacia on the relatively high hill higher than the sudden hill we pass in the car, that abandoned dump. Suspense is exhausting but inexhaustible—and it is insolent, perhaps because it thrives on the insufficiencies of the present, the untenability of our prospects for the future.

One can't be a scholar of the future, one can't learn from it, one can't even learn about it. You think it's a man in the distance coming along the country road, but as Husserl remarks, "it might be a tree moving in the wind, which in the gloom of the late afternoon at the edge of the field resembles a man in motion." We define things by their peripheries, their proximities, the things around them to which they are bound but from which they differ. Trust has little to do with it; we cast out tendrils of interpretation as if with a paranoiac's perspicacity and lucidity. "You utter fools, you senseless people," says Sophocles's Old Slave in *Electra*, "do you take no heed any longer for your lives, or have you no inborn sense, that you fail to see that you are not merely close to but are in the midst of the greatest dangers?" To establish the character and value of something, we negotiate with the future, we barter with what we think we see ahead, what we expect to come. We traffic in what we hope for, what we fear, what we can't finish by ourselves.

"AGATHON OF THE BEAUTIFUL VERSES is about to set the pegs on which to frame the play." Here the beautiful Agathon, author of lost tragic verses, is a character in a comedy. Here for a moment and then, time being what it is (whatever it is), we have only his name and rumor with its subsequent commotion. Aristophanes continues: "He is bending new curves for his verses; he is chiseling some bits, fixing some with song-glue, knocking up maxims, making periphrases, wax-moulding, rounding, casting." The comedian is always in motion, dancing to the staccato beat of disarray—motion is the genius of comedy, its reality. While that beautiful Agathon in his elegance prepares a song long with the legato of catastrophe, Aristophanes laughs. It's tragedies that unfold in the aftermath of the collisions that cause history, but the grand profusion when everything comes out at the end is sheer comedy.

Five city pigeons fly into the air, driven from their perch under the eaves of a gray house by a homeowner bombarding them with tennis balls. A disheveled man goes by pulling a wagon and shouting curses to the curb and then to the corner store. Brotherfuck mothermouth turd-on-a-rock-in-your-face, do you hear me, do you hear me? Definitely—one should nurture one's private sensibility (one's "inner life"). One should deploy it in social spaces, pitch in, speak up, participate in "public life." You can belong where you are for a moment. When everything gets loud enough—which is to say when sounds coalesce into a din—everything achieves synchrony, orchestration, and synonymy.

All in due course the arid dust in one place receives recompense from incoming rains and heavy floods in another are lifted from gray sodden fields by a dry dazzling wind. For a moment, both feet of justice are on the ground; on the hillside above the path through the park the buckeyes balance pink and white blossoms on clublike stalks. I assume there's some determinate character to the reality of the moment—something necessary, something causing or compelling things of the moment to be real. Or, rather, to appear. But everything to this point has been the product of guesswork, like improvised masonry done on dry days through weeks of a wet winter or electrical wiring done by an amateur, and no doubt will be long after it. Along the median strip the hardies, the perennials, the continuing, are back: penstemons and sages, poppies and lavender, street people and day laborers. The stoplights flicker; a rock falls onto the edge of the highway—a rock with a pinkish-orange hue close to the color of a fallen peach in dust. Despite all the violence and crime inherent to tragedy, every tragedy also includes innocence. Each character makes its appearance but none are backed by a narrative, nor am "I"—I appear like all the others, unnarrativized, unstoried, on the margins of ambiguity. To live aesthetically—to live in terms of, to live in the contexts and limits of, the phenomenal world (and perhaps interpretations of it)—to live facing *outward* (without "seizing" or "capturing" or otherwise "possessing" phenomena): this is to live in terms of surfaces. Things surface, thoughts come to the surface, etc. And it's not just there that we find something as indeterminate as a ricochet, something erratic, demanding decision, something for which we or you or I or she or they or one or he or someone has to take responsibility. In a burst of enthusiasm, I embarrass myself with a burst of enthusiasm. So be it: acts of synthesizing consciousness can produce "complete distinctness of 'logical' understanding," which, however, can "pass over into vagueness."

In a book such as this (whatever kind of book it is such of), typically the narrator—a given "I"—would have introduced an erotic element—a drive, a yearning so fundamental and unavoidable as to feel instinctual, intuitive: a feeling above all of feeling. But let's set aside questions of kind, category, etc.—this is not a book in search of a genre, though genres may come searching for it or creep over some of its phrases. There's no truth to identity. At best it's subjunctive, not indicative. I pick up a pen—passionately, say—and, not yet even knowing what words will appear, I begin to write: subjectivity (personality) emanates from intoxication.

The phenomenal world is what there is—material particulars, happenstantial circumstances, everyday life—why speak of futurity, a metaphysical imposition, an empty category into which anything might enter but nothing has? Perhaps we do so because it offers prospects of what's ahead far from the importunate past and—this may be key—without promises. The forces of eros, the barbs and bewilderments, the obliterating passions and (dare we say) pulsations—the relentless throbbing and irritable insistences—of eros (and let's not limit eroticism just to sex) may be ubiquitous, they may be banal, but let's credit them with pushing us along, taking us, for example, on yet another "intellectual promenade." "With stopovers"—nominal, adverbial, prepositional, participial. *Street drunkenly twig for gab compatibly starch*. Every word is an iteration, each testing for something—accuracy? insight? truth (whatever that might be)?—seeking "successively closer approximations to the solution of a problem." And there it is: skepticism makes too many demands. Lola is never overly eager to join together things that have no connections and with that to create a story pitting fate against fact, but what of clowns, tightrope walkers, a lion tamer, a parade of elephants? I don't buy that they're shadow forms under a big top—they're feeling points, they're proximities. Animated by sudden, worldbound, outfacing feelings, Lola laughs with both hands in the air: here's to the raptures of proximity! Names are given heavy with hidden insistence generating an epistemology of given moments in and of the phenomenal world, the given and apparent world of the historical present, said to be a system, said to prohibit off-cycle harvests, said to be in the eye of a temporal maelstrom, said to be the last thing basking in sunlight at the end-time. Jewassi Zhdanov Jones swings right from the last daylight on Chant Street into the white-walled bar, she's quickly crafted, or, since this is a social occasion, she's already sitting at a table with Jamie Brecht Weiss, Freya Cyprian Slight, Rosie Consuela Hassan, and Lola: she's quickly performed, immediate as a being in a continuous take of eternal duration. But it's not as if everyday life were forever static and ahistorical—as if a single scoop of chocolate ice cream on a sugar cone were always to cost a dime, humans were to forage forever in hills and on plains to the edge of the terrestrial flat finite disk, or someone first called Silly couldn't later and emphatically be known as Priscilla Salter Blaine with Pris banned flat out. Let's imagine a city pigeon in harness presented as an allegorical image captioned "The Life of the Mind," a punctum perceived amid "tangents and repetitions and intersections."

When doubt recedes, they say, it's death that approaches to drive a wedge between meaning and its trappings, its contradictions, its digressions and confusions as well as its minnows, fern spores, ladles, architectural renderings of commercial towers, stained-glass windows, manifestos, curries. Of course one can imagine death as rapacious, greedy, an impatient predator, a scavenger charged with clean-up, or, then again, as a supreme and theatrical deity, over-inked or underground. Well, as a skeptic once put it, it's wisest to follow the principle of *the one no more than the other,* which is as applicable to interpretations of allegory as to personifications of death. The thought—a proposition, or perhaps a phantasm drawn from an impression—serves a sentence. There isn't all that much distance between the prospect of death and the concept of beauty. A ridge, a sunset, a blossoming redbud—all are beautiful and, in their beauty, they assert their distance from us, but even today's unvarying dull sky maintains distance, as if to make beauty itself inaccessible. The rain has stopped, low to the ground there's fog—Floka pulls the hood of her raincoat back, Tasha her dog is off-leash and sniffs at dripping trees, wet hummocks, soggy soil under dark amorphous leaves.

On a battlefield (whether literal or metaphoric), humans encounter the problem of humanity: what is the *value* to being human? Call a character an exasperated chemist, Max Marie Ritter, and Max Marie Ritter will have retorts to clean, carbon to consider, big pharma to advise, and mockery to make of boy groups, mayonnaise, house cats, and conspiracy theories. Characters are necessary to human microhistories, but those histories are of what has happened and is happening and not revelations of intelligent inevitability nor milestones along a road to progress. Along with the plethora of interconnected phenomena come experiences of disconnection. Why isn't it always summer? Pilar Piana Fleye isn't asking a question, she's complaining, demanding rays of attention. You never know why, says Milly Willis. And about this Milly Willis is right: those who love logic are apt to love lies. What case, then, can we make for human understanding?

ALMOST—that unfinished bridge, that unfinished part of it—adds inconclusive, mild suspense to a project, plan, or intention; it is the failure immanent in perception. *Almost* marks perception's ultimate imprecision. Or so it seems. But perhaps imprecision and inconclusiveness are among the achievements of our senses, perhaps *almost* is the condition of immanence in thought, like the pause between exhalation and breathing in. Possibility, imagination, irrationality can enter and set their logic, time is a toy, duty stops in its tracks. Milly Margaret Willis perceives that, deprived by old age of the right to be listened to, she is no longer considered a source of info or opinion, she has no user name, no password, no log-in. She's thinking she should concentrate ruthlessly when encountering a rock or tree—she's thinking of the park—or pond algae or—looking out the window—a string of cyclists in skin-tight cycling suits, each rising slightly off their seat as they sweep over a curb to protect that ever-unforgettable place between the legs. Unlike a skeptic, the old perceiver wants to make a confession, as if that would bring about some kind of conclusion or at least give her some friends and restore her psychosocial resilience—as if it would restore her to a place in the world, as if it would let her voice be a part again in the choral hum of the city's sounds. She wants to be a unit of experience.

Zander Blue Dallas, with an IPA, a bowl of pretzels, and something on his mind, and Enrico Wren Roberts, bringing me a chardonnay and carrying a beer, come back to the faux wood table, its narrow edge abutting the rosy wall. Beyond them the room is taking on the warm hues, if not the symbolism, of a worn Kashan rug—the room is emanating a robin-russet polychrome of asymmetrical calm, profound perfected irrelevance—and that's the point. What did you get? Just the usual, says Enrico: the Hazy IPA. Thought goes into a name and thought should come out of it, adding to a social field, a city, say, with playgrounds and small parks, and miles of hilly or wooded parks along its eastern edge, all in focus now that spring is near though belied by rain that's ameliorating the drought—for now. On the screen above the bar a baseball game is underway on mute; the camera is trained on Ben "Blister" Baxter, the team's primary pitching commodity, I know that much, and it's time to lighten up, it's no tragedy to have lived a long time, and aging, after all, is just another madcap adventure. Twentieth-century cartoons, satirically or not, depict moments of pathos; they are the twentieth century's version of nineteenth-century sentimental genre painting. The camera pans the crowd and then zooms in on a sample fan, an exuberant child waving a cowboy hat, we see Blister at bat, the camera follows the ball, Blister flails, recovers, and stands like an off-season upright robin on schmaltzy, treacherous ground. It's not the present that binds the past to the future—the present is an anomaly, even an anachronism; between "an open future and an unrepeatable past" there's incessant motion—the proverbial flash, flutter, and flicker and, for the sake of more alliteration, the flinching. Stuff and its interpretation remain perpetually on loan to each other, each presenting intransigent signs—pennants, we might call them, purposive, proprietary signs. Do I imagine, create—do I *think* these things—in the key of dream, in the fantasies of fiction? And where do they come from: are they sparked by eavesdropping, produced by observations, spun out of surmise, served up as the dubious brew we call memory? What is the germ of this corruption, this unreality? Nietzsche has it yet again: "The more insight we possess into an origin the less significant does the origin appear."

Calling geese in formation are flying overhead, northward more or less (as if going down Flats Street but 1,000 feet above it), but perhaps they're going only as far as the old artificial body of water on Grand Lake in the next city over, eliciting not a picture—not an image, insofar as convention equates image with something visualized, even when that image is initiated (prompted, sparked) by a sound or odor or texture or taste—but an event in the ear, a sequence of notes, a set of sounds and the movements that organize them into something particular even if it's disorganized, a cacophony, separate moments becoming one moment, uncaptured, so experienced perhaps rather than imagined. What would we come up with if asked for a semantic analysis of this rough V of geese in flight (it's already mutating), or of the outspread moment of the flock's quacks and honking borne into a unit of sonic consciousness, and why not call that too an image, isn't admitting experience into consciousness a work of imagination, after all? Into consciousness but not necessarily cognition. It's in the nature of human cognition to be influenced, and much of the time this goes on unconsciously—humans are sweepingly inattentive, not least because to be all-attentive would require round-the-clock work: whatever we might mean by the term semantics, none of it is universally or perpetually valid; concepts and, even more to the point, names are just detaining positions. Lola is tucked into a job as a junior analytic cartographer of the city's built underworld sunk and snuggled into the terrain of microbes, worms, burrowing bugs, disintegrating debris, roots, stones, seeds, gophers, and ash.

The future takes many things away even before we get to them, but not knowing what they might have been we don't—we can't—give a thought to them. We will return to the perplexing existence of thought in due course. Meanwhile, though many futures are effaced from futurity, already existing futures proliferate all around us; the planet, despite the ruination that is spreading over it, still provides plenty of fertile ground. And there—I mean *here*—mischievous as an aeronautic penis, cunning as an aqueous cunt—the powerful as well as pesky instruments of reproduction are at work (or is it play?), potentially if not certainly providing stuff for an ever-expanding future and the eventual vastation of the universe. This is not the *luxe, calme et volupté* that Baudelaire imagined at some voyage's end amidst glowing stones polished by years: witness the sociality at sundown of baboons.

My literary-perceptual studies began early, Tony van Heuvel is saying—(he hears the pomposity in this and leans slightly back in his chair)—I guess it was in ninth grade, I pompously (he's nipping the problem in the bud, so to speak—he's dodging it)—I pompously committed myself to a daily *analytico-descriptive* project—a fancy term that I certainly couldn't have come up with at the time—I guess it was a kind of *thought experiment*: my idea was to practice until I could make my vision razor sharp and my words even sharper—is that a male thing: sword and razor play? Is his self-awareness evidence of modesty or arrogance, Tamarind Magee wonders—something like that; she likes Tony van Heuvel. I'd describe one of my teachers at the blackboard, say, or a security guard smoking outside a Wells Fargo bank—I definitely remember that guy—or a mixed-breed pit bull tied to a parking meter outside the library, and then—this was the hard part—just by adding an adverb, that was the rule, I'd try to show how that particular teacher, security guard, or dog resembles no other. Stately, plump preliminary, Tamarind says—does -ly make stately an adverb? Razor and mirror, Tony says—*Ulysses* is built entirely of signifying practices. Tamarind Magee looks up and gestures toward the room. She's right: social space (here of the café) comes into being as a space of performances, sure, but (she realizes) also of something more fundamental that is only immanent in the performances but becomes the meaning-structure of the whole space, the feeling-structure of the piece.

Say this is a day devoted to the sound of rain, or to the whole obscure—the whole obscuring—genius of rain. Well, not entirely—but the rain is drawing attention to itself repeatedly, though so too does the question, the quandary even, since the rain is falling heavily and doesn't seem to be letting up and there aren't any salad greens or eggs in the fridge and there's only a glassful or less of wine left in the bottle from last night (maybe this is the most salient deficit, the telling deh-fee-*seet* [just so the word so often heard in the once-and-gone USSR comes to mind])—of what to cook for dinner tonight and when to go out for what's needed. What would Heraclitus or the woman whose mummified body fell into an Irish peat bog twenty-five thousand years ago think of this, our human present, what would Caesar make of it, what would Sappho, what would Karl Marx? Marilyn Monroe—or, if we want to stay in the realm of the dramatico-fictional, Dame Quickly—might take a look around and be "tickled to death," she might "laugh until she cries" or, alternatively, she might "laugh until she pees in her pants." History—the purported record cum interpretation of past events and conditions—is always naïve, epically naïve. It's vastly insufficient, copiously oblivious, naïve to the point of insensibility: where are all the overlooked figures, where are the unrecorded and forgotten names, where are the banal, ordinary, trivial, quotidian essentials? The question itself, or the complaint implicit to it, is itself banal. Human history is that of the zombies we've become—as must be the case: the lived feeling for and of the past is always only a lived feeling for the present that is (naïvely) imagining it and all now is performed in the key of banality. But what did we expect, everything?

The wind blusters, the setting sun swirls around battleship-gray passing clouds. That's all wrong, of course—it's the planet that's turning away from the sun and the clouds are passing above and below it—but just as there are thoughts one can't think, thoughts that humans don't have brain or mind for, there are thoughts we can think (and do), even though they are the products of language—imaginative concepts leading to perceptual errors and perceptual pleasures. But I'm just puffing out loud now like a passenger train on passing tracks whistling through an empty intersection, but it's thus that we'll get to the problem of thought. Thought: a dark European railroad station seen through billowing steam the color of dandelion fluff (an incongruous association, but incongruities are often the best things' thinking spots). A melancholy water tower stalwart in a landscape of perpetually blowing dust, alone except for the bolstering presence of sturdy cacti and the meaningless drift of rat-gray tumbleweed. There are dingy hills in the background—perhaps something will come out of them. Before humans had movies to teach them how to dream from one thing to another, there were fires to stare into and rivers to wade in, to paddle up, to float down, or to just watch. Clouds too, but not just visible things, quick or slow to change—there were the ever-modulating frog and cricket choruses to dream with, the toad in the dark that hailed one by the wrong name, the wind moving from fir trees to oaks to madrone. Instead of divine magic acts, we got metamorphoses—and, in due course, dial tones in A.

IT'S HARD TO IMAGINE MONDAYS as zones of continuity, it's hard to pick up where the weekend as such leaves off and go on with the business of continuing. "Stories that are fragmented, non-linear, impressionistic and contingent are better suited than traditional linear narratives to the experience of walking in ruins"—so a cultural geographer has said. Elsewhere and on a different day, a musicologist has described an "extended quartet" as sounding like "a bottle blown by a saxophone"; "extended," but that might infer "pernicious" or, on the other hand, "monumental." It's all a matter of context, which is to say chance: the bottle might have been shattered. *Blunder watch do is for closely language on*. Lola challenges art to justify itself with some perceptible point to its story. Clearly there's no point in applying poetry to itself or to war, she says. I acquiesce, it being the duty—it being the *right*—of the old to yield to the young in a family. Maybe the point of historicism it is not that it looks to the past for an understanding of the present but that, in looking to the past, it seeks to pause the present—to save it from itself.

Things might have been otherwise. Maybe that should be inscribed over the door to every museum, on the spine of every book, over the stage of every performance hall and movie theater. Past the top of the four-sided tower at the edge of the plaza there's an inkling of a falcon, then clouds to break the monotony. Incompletely, artworks emerge from proliferating trajectories, harboring memories and other unlikelihoods including that of art itself. I say they emerge incompletely—that's because completion is not something artworks can achieve. A work of art is always social and always necessarily a product of its epoch, but other epochs (and other places) will inevitably enter into its making, as forces, influences, and materials and also as outcomes and alternatives—futures. Eternally?—that's way too much. As for historical reality: let's compare it to skin blemishes; political systems: let's compare them to gruel. The vitality of what we might call a *moment of art* is apt to decrease as we begin to suspect that everything is futile. What's bewildering is not imagination nor even interpretation, which imagination propels—one can almost always backtrack and deconstruct those. The inexplicable as well as unextractable activity is *thinking*. And in the wake of thinking lie thoughts, impenetrable, mineral—thinking's past tense cast into the present. The entirety of John Coltrane's *Ascension* is one thought, Cezanne's *Still Life with Apples* is many, Coleridge's "This Lime-Tree Bower My Prison" depicts more thinking than thoughts. In the café, Reggie Clara Toss is staying on task, adding "Impossible Burger (plant not beef)" to the listings on the menu board behind the counter.

Exercising one's freedom, one chooses how to respond to necessity. But this isn't a true choice; one chooses not what to do but only the means and/or manner of doing it. It's a rare necessity that leaves no options. At some point we'll get caught in the act of trying to redistribute or recirculate subjectivity. After all, each of us is just one bit of interpreted stuff in the throes of interpreting amid myriads of other bits doing the same. Move the rocking chair, sound the alarm, with infamous anonymity help yourself to ice cream. Reality is a given, whatever it comprises. Or, to phrase that differently, we designate what is commonly apparent to what we deem reality, if for no better reason than that we have to do so for practical purposes, but in the process the apparent loses its tenuousness; it acquires the intransigence we associate with tyranny. So let's here introduce the kitchen pantry, painted off-white and presented upside down with all its stuff tumbling up (now down) willy-nilly; the paltry objects of quotidian life are staging a protest; a jar of marmalade is supporting a box of penne.

Language, like the wrinkling sea, is a satirical success with "the power to wield negatives" over the oceanic materiality of the phenomenal world. It changes names, and things, beings, disappear from the already concealed story as a pedigree might from the ears of a spayed family mutt named Tasha. Named, nameless, renamed, misnamed: one still cannot be the organizer or stager of the event we call *void*, the drama we call an *abyss*. Overhead the sky in the scattered light is a pale blue, less an energy field, despite the season, than a placid presence, without ego, act, content, object. How satisfying it must be in this context to come upon the noun at the end of a line (it might be *dredge, accident, list,* it might be *fate, finesse,* or *doom*) and believe that the supreme rebuttal to history is poetry. And if a line or two or three later we come upon *wedge, provident, twist* or *crate, duress,* or *elbow room,* could we credibly claim that language is proving that where we think we find coincidence we are instead encountering convergence, and that the convergence produces synchrony, transcendent as the vividly anachronistic? No, but how appealing it once seemed, the mystical nonsense about the numinous power of language, which in fact would have condemned us from the start to "a hell of eternal interpretation." No doubt it would have been waged in the name of freedom—but for what? The problem of knowing how to situate oneself in its labyrinth of possibilities could bring one to the point of doubting one's very existence.

In front of his house, Monty Michael Leary continues his battle with the pigeons roosting under the eaves, watching for a break in the traffic and then throwing carefully aimed tennis balls at the perched birds from the middle of Rusty Street. Looking out beyond the surface-bound and space-shy shadows playing over the pavement and curb under the streetside sycamore tree, sits an errant glowing buttercup edged in black—it's not alone in the landscape of fringed objectivity and displays no compulsion to flaunt understanding. There it is over oval, dark green leaves—flagrant in the current context (the dreary square of exposed ground left free for a tree when the sidewalk was laid), vulnerable to the piss or shit of a dog, bright on a random Wednesday, Odin's day or Mercury's. We should be amazed—we should have the energy for that and the attention span. As for a paragraph like this one—here it sits in the least object-oriented of the arts, full not of things but of a language for things.

And yet the infamous gap between word and world is usually little more than a crack, a squiggle through a surface, a delicate fissure, a reminder that language is an addition to, not a murky substitute for, the scrutable world. The crack is for real, though—depending on size or inclination, one can step into it or step over it. In the process, understanding is suspended, knowledge drops, but a crack in the ground—even a crack right through it—is not meaning's abyss. Ask any cow about unstable grounds or any goose about uncertain terms and she'll agree, like any mother applying herself to a place in a field, forest, ocean, tidepool, or room whether she's a doe, a hen, a bitch, a mare, lioness, ewe, jenny, vixen, nanny, jill, peahen, hind, dam, tigress, angeline, woman, or sow. We're not talking about resignation to uncertainty here, and it's not fortitude in the face of the inevitable either, though both resignation and fortitude may be required now and then—when making sense of situations, conditions, or even happenstantial occurrences (flash floods, moldy yogurt, a splinter under the skin) one has to negotiate with reality, and reality can be quirky. It's definitely frisky, though sometimes slowly so. It's only with immortality—if that's what comes at the end of mortality—irrevocable absence, incomprehensible nonbeing—that the gap between words and world reveals meaning's abyss, the impossibility not only of objectivity but of objects, things whose sense has got to be shared, the stuff of sociality. And without that the present exits. And possibility, like freedom, ceases to be an applicable metaphysical concept.

Houses and small (four- and five-story) apartment buildings stand in the way of the hills. We want the hills to break through, to become visible, bringing their bushes, grasses, trees, dun hummocks, and gray rocks with them, we want the hills back. Or we want the visibility of the hills back, liberated from the dense material façades that wall them in—or out. They were here long before human thought with its overvalued lyric overlay of longing and its infrastructuring narratives ("constitutive illusions") of past frustrations and future flights. "Nondescript," "scrubby"?—anyone alert to their senses knows that the city streets and those worn, consequential foothills, as well as the local farmlands and interlocking state parks, are sites of strange, contributing, contradictory facts, quiddities, phenomena, and situations harboring extraordinary, sometimes inexplicable, bizarre, and even sublime things. Strange—my relationship to the world isn't lyric, and yet I give myself freedom for contingency and, more important, freedom *in* it, too. That's only relative freedom, though—freedom exercised, not given.

PARMENIDES IN HIS GREAT POEM, in order (so he claims) to inoculate his audience against the misleading marvels and debilitating falsities of *mere appearance* so that humans will seek appearance's contrary, *true reality* (or, more simply, *truth*), exposes them to an account of what he views as delusional appearances—the entirety of the phenomenal world under and including "the common aether and Milky Way and the outermost heaven and the hot strength of the stars" that "thrust forward" and the moon in the sky, "Night-shiner, wandering around the earth, an alien light / Always looking towards the rays of the sun." These are among the things he sees and describes (but fails to debunk, at least to an anti-Platonist like me) as he begins his picaresque journey in a chariot drawn by mares across "a threshold of stone" and through "the gates of Night and Day." Some two millennia later, abandoning theological in favor of secular grounds for choosing what and how to paint, major (mostly Dutch) artists of the seventeenth century turned away from portraits of aristocrats, depictions of saints, and battle scenes and took up the portrayal of landscapes featuring undulating mud (stone has melted away) and miniscule people (no goddess or Parmenides here)—"a landscape," as Lytle Shaw puts it, "where humans and their dramas are not the primary concern," and where the ground slows itself into the pleasure of appearance and the scandal of its obviousness. Does *amor fati* curtail freedom or merely slow it? Let's say it does both—that's the easy way out, and in any case it's neither fate nor appearances (or *amor apparentiae*) but love that limits things, feelings are what configure all that we perceive, feeling itself is probably the very first of our percepts. And soon there's mud, applesauce, and more and more to come. But I can't blame the future for the wanderings of my attention, despite the fact that curiosity, hope, promises, aspiration, and love all depend on the prospect of a future: I have happily let the future seduce me into promiscuous interpreting, blissful guesswork, centrifugal speculation, and wayward propositions.

Back on the ground, the present plants its moments. Leo X. Lee looks to his right at the crisp black cab of a Chevy Silverado shuddering to the visceral throb of an amped-up bass to which the young blond woman behind the wheel seems oblivious. Midnight in the sorority, he says to Tamarind Magee. Can't use it, she says, old news, a false lead, thumb on the hammer. Over Flats Ave there's a thin blue sky and pale sunlight brushes the rooftops and hillsides, yesterday's dark massive clouds having melted away during the night, swirling down the sewer drains or sinking into the ground.

Characters and concepts, moments and anachrony, events and emptiness (not to mention the international dateline that traverses the Pacific from north to south and back again and divides the future from the past): everyday life in the mind as well as on the ground is rife with contradictions. And we have no outside knowledge of ourselves, we can't see ourselves, we don't know what we look like, how we move, we don't know if we have bad breath—and where's the survival value in all this? Humans have a delusional love of power (King of the Jungle, Queen of All the Russias, Lord of the Rings, Lord of the Flies, etc.), they either want power or they abjectly cater to it or quake at its knees or they collectively revel in hating the powerful and that shared hatred is a source of power in itself. But it's spring and artichokes are back on the shelves at the market, a few wearing an oval sticker saying KISSED BY FROST in Helvetica, all caps, black ink. Haha: Rosie Consuela Hassan is texting. The still bee continues as space speeds by in the leafy air of time. The rupture between microcosm and macrocosm disappears.

ESSE
WUPP
SELDORF
KÖLN
Sieg
LAHN
excit
often found
daunting m
the Societ
shamelessly pop
offers Orff
Teem
A509
B127

FOUR

Paradise can make itself scarce,
that's the way of it.
CHRISTA WOLF

METAMORPHOSIS is a shifty recurrence: dust off a robin at one minute and an opal in oatmeal the next with nothing but disappearance between. That's the ticket, that's why poems take line breaks. It's harder for prose to counterpunch its stories, nearly impossible for data science to part with superstition. April yard mice and off-leash dogs move around in their respective forms of life and humans move around in theirs, guided by assumptions and bound to social mores, narratives of the way things have to be. Yellow sourgrass, like memory with its circuit of dispatches, dissensions, dead ends, and perilous accords, clings to the deceptive surface of the continental crust high above meandering faults between plates afloat on liquid stone.

But did you say omelet or omniscience when referring to the sun? Dream on, the sun sets, give reason a rest. There's ample evidence here of the ongoing incoherence of the real underfoot, the roots, gophers, rivulets, ditches, stones, worms. And when the sun comes up, look at the greens—their mobility! With a crash of breaking glass the Reco-Volution truck collects its weekly haul of recyclable bottles, jars, cans, plastic, cardboard, and paper from the blue bins set against the curb. As for what really happens to all that stuff: how do they define *recycled*? Or amor fati—an inquiry into that can't help but acknowledge absurdity, its jovial duplicities, its inefficient ways of getting from A to B, its scattershot preponderance and irrelevant reveries.

Bonnie Rose Roberts and (yet to appear) Tina, Colette, and Giselle: they are names noisy with friendship, inflated with play. To interpret their game is to play the clown in the ghost, to press the wrinkle on the lips. Guess that's just the way it is, as Leo X. Lee says: improv—interpretation is irrepressible, magical, a conduit of ecstasy. In its long riff on absurdity, it can't be stopped. As for love—and this, after all, is what Bonnie, Tina, Colette, and Giselle are learning to play—it puts a limit on human understanding and can't outlive it. The benign perplexity, the gently uncomprehending look—these are gestures in the *mise-en-scène*, pieces of necessary equipment when playing for friendship and playing with love. The performance yields a set of anecdotes and observations intended to exemplify how a being—a person, character, figure, human, creature, maybe even a thing—means itself: what each intends or what each feels intended *as* and *for*. Giselle Hugo Roy looks up at the dark fir tree near the edge of the park as if it were a meteor or Mont Blanc, achieving sudden sublimity and entering her repertoire of fantasies, secret but not introspective. Complete—completely virtuous—objectivity is impossible; it's beyond language's capabilities; face it, it's beyond all of us. Giselle is experiencing powerful emotions in response to realizing that she is experiencing powerful emotions. And if subjectivity is, in fact, always inter-subjectivity, isn't this only because one is subjectified by being objectified, made perceptible, and isn't it the case that around every subjectivity there's an impenetrable boundary, love, making it impossible for one ever to be fully known or fully understood by someone else, by anyone? An unusual wind is coming up, pushing a low layer of battle-ash gray clouds, darkening the sky and dulling the moment; shadows are disappearing as ghosts might near the paradoxically light-dark end of a novel beset by an ambiguous allegorical (or otherworldly) atmosphere. Under the tree like a cyber-serious super-sensing dog sits a single shoe. I'm over here, Bonnie calls, and Giselle runs toward her; Giselle does not yet quite have the monologic perspective that social mores will make automatic; she does not yet ask how it would be if others see things as she does.

Conscious beings picture things into situations, conditions, events, and we can call the picturing faculty interpretation, imagination, or contextualization, etc., each of which brings with it its own nuances, limits, and possibilities. Say, for example, that there's a cat on the desk and she's slinking toward me, undulating with earnestness—she's providing social interference, in command of her soft exigencies which, inviting no force, force us to respond as one might from an incoming tide. Does yesterday's story change in today's context or is yesterday's story the context that is today? As the great classicist R. B. Onians, writing on Hesiod's *Works and Days*, observes, "The day has a certain quality, gives something, and he who is wise cooperates by acting so as to receive the good and avoid the evil." But what about invitations—even one's invitations to oneself—invitations to something and to some end? I admit that I seem always to be wanting to make something, a mark, a line, a move. "It is given to me" or "I'm called upon," etc.—but just how passive is the invitee and how active, even activist, is the inviter? "I" marks a fault line, the potential for disturbance or one might say the dangerous space of compulsion or of the desire for possibility. Each day is a mystery that can never be solved; it is never empty and always governing change—and, of course, interminable change is all that we have of outcomes.

When writing by hand Placo Paris Wang, "the February detective," doesn't close his o's, he keeps them open, ambiguous, demonstrative, *au courant*. The point is to activate milieu perception and disconnect it from an obsession with private property. Materia Tamayo-Cole laughs without pleasure: Placo dude, get real. I'm talking about holding patterns—that's the sort of thing Placo might say in reply, and I know what he's thinking: I'm making him up. As the making goes, so does Placo Paris Wang. There's nothing intrinsically wrong with a love of solitude and the exercising of inwardness, but weaponized as instruments of individualism and declared to be a fundamental right—that's where the danger begins. And that's where detection comes in.

The horizon is woven low and hanging far and apart; it's unearthly—no place for a tragedian, no place for an archeologist. The ground is detection's fallen wall. Casting a thin wavering shadow a nasturtium leaf on its wide heretical pad extends an interrogatory green. Every question is like a "shaky island of impious upheaval"—the phrase is seized as if it were quarry and, worse, misquoted. Statements and stories proliferate, humans thrive in a lie, we're out of this world, realities are supplanted, new truths develop, these, in turn, generate new fictions, and so on and so forth, old if not fake news. Sure, fantasy is false facticity in this don't-look-down and if-you-say-it-then-it's-true world. But how hard is it, really, and how bad would it be, to imagine that the incoming tide is like a liquid sheet of beaten egg whites or like the ululations of a woman in mourning or like the sensations of a little girl on a swing all in innocence getting a lesson on the sexual profundity of the rise and spill?

The sky above appears blue. Or it might be gold—apparently some see it so—or green or gray: the aging sky, wrinkled and old, bearing scars from its many, its multiple, days. Crossed by birds, covered by clouds, coveted by towers or by architects of towers. Builders of cathedrals, meanwhile, seek to lower the sky, to bring it close. And look at how the sky itself in Giotto's "Rising of Lazarus" descends, a sky (as T. J. Clark puts it) "so absolute and terrestrial" as to bring its blue to ground.

AH—ENTER THE SPRING MOUSE! The cat hasn't wasted her patience; now cruelly she toys, her claws like commas, her tail exclamatory. She's engaged in an old crime, or it's an old game to the very last detail, but it's never exactly the same; let's call her Chardonnay. We build our nests with commas; adding stuff, adjusting things; our nests are riddled with commas and, at the risk of sounding glib, they are riddled *by* them. Think how readily—how all but automatically—our sympathies lie at hand to solve the riddle of life. What should we anticipate, and how should we do it, and where—in the conviviality of a social space or under the bed? We live in a universe of instances and details, yes, but not separated from each other, not in isolation. But doesn't this—the notion of "inseparable details" and confluent instances—generalize them, deprive details of their detail and sever instances from their instantiations? That is a rhetorical question, mischievously masking a proposition.

Lola just doesn't seem like the horsey type, says Freya Cyprian Slight. Try cowgirl. Cowgirl? With irony. With no fear, says Noor; the correction is adamant. With rhetorical flourish, says Andre Micah Blake; he points to the door of the bar and the sunlit sidewalk in front of it and Lola appears, dashing and jocular in devilish Western garb: she's wearing tight black jeans, a black-embroidered long-sleeve snap-front shirt, a black Stetson with a blue headband, and black round-top cowboy boots with whimsical blue stitching. And wit, adds Andre. Rhetoric! says Lola. She kisses Andre on the cheek—rhetoric is a cave and here we are—hurray—we've retreated into it to escape our total destruction.

Though farce happens, it's unfated: it doesn't happen *to* anyone, rather someone happens into *it*, whereas tragedy always happens to someone—or to many; as for comedy: it's all around, all at once, everywhere. Tragedy produces stasis, immobility, plutonic impenetrability and permanence; the tragedies are petrified by fate. But, though histories may end there, real life doesn't always do so: even when involving raging catastrophe, comedy moves on, stumbling through catastrophe's ubiquitous debris—its blazing rubble, rotting heads, twisted signs. The comical trudge—note how closely weeping resembles laughter; they yodel to tune the bassoon, and sing a song to bring on the sun. The farcical propose—they take a leap of faith, *saltus fidei*, meant to fool fate and chase its witnesses away. Propositions are like randy satyrs in a mere game of war taking characteristically brilliant and provocative plunges into the woods. They are the rogues, out and about, impetuous, free for lack of evidence, vivaciously aprowl, insouciant survivors of reality checks, and provoking just the right feel of rightness. There's a sudden sensation, a demanding twinkle or twinge on the chin, a bite, an itch, and I scratch it—I'm a ready target. Compared to aphorisms, which are propositions amplified with apostrophic elements, bare propositions are pitiless. "Combining entertainment with instruction in the most natural manner" (as Pat Rogers says of Boswell's *Life of Johnson*), aphorisms frolic, though whether they cavort out of bile, in rage, frustration, and intellectual disgust or out of delight, sheer energy, and mirth depends on the mood of the *aphoriste*, and the mood of the *aphoriste* depends on more than I can possibly know. It's said that aphorisms require interpretation; propositions, on the other hand, are often the culmination of interpretation. But, as should be evident, interpreting some aphorisms is like conducting a séance with a mobster. The pro is a con, as Andre Micah Blake would say. Sincerity can only go so far; insincerity can go only a little further.

Pythagoras (it's been said) accused Homer of lying about the gods after Pythagoras in a vision saw what he took to be Homer in what he took to be Hades suffering the torments properly inflicted on liars: teeth as hot as coals burning in a pit, tongue on fire, larynx liquifying. Homer, however, is a composite figure, an idea, a name in place of a person—a social being *par excellence*. According to Diogenes Laertius's account, Pythagoras "told of the wanderings of his soul, how it migrated hither and thither, into how many plants and animals it had come, and all that it underwent in Hades, and all that the other souls there have to endure." Pythagoras was a sequential being with alter egos experienced in a series of reincarnations under different names; let us imagine that he remembered not as a witness but as each being he was: he remembered as wisteria, as a bullock, as Euphorbus (wounded, according to Homer in the *Iliad*, by Menelaus), without any false subjectivities along the way. But Homer had far greater social literacy than Pythagoras.

A child, emerging from infancy and for the first time negotiating stairs, ascends earnestly, strenuously, focusing on the climb, but the descent?—an ascent in reverse?—headfirst? No—first toe and foot then knee go first: the descent is a preliminary to walking, or, to put it another way, all walking is a descent. The social world is behind the child—like a goat or cat the child climbs, like a raptor, kite, or like heat he or she rises. And then down the child goes, pursuing perpendicular thinking, launching him- or herself on a study of clue burial, set on a course of detection; the social world is waiting. The ground is suddenly interesting. Fleas, dog shit, plastic lids, twigs cast down from trees, an infant's sock on the curb, the commas scattered through prose—the substrate of civilization, its dust, dirt, and debris. And waves of subjectivity, the flow of subjects with their spears, apricots, underpants, food allergies, and shoes. We can't liberate the surface from what's on it, but we can scratch at mute materiality and poke at faint memory. There we have it: all mood and freedom and phenomena all around, uncontained by either beauty, reason, longing, or knowledge; we are thrust into a lyrical existence by the senses.

Unfolding scenarios of sparking or decimated love, transcendent intensifications of vitality or unruly crushing of the spirit, lay down their histories, but memories of those periods of exuberance or desolation are the stuff of present time while the feelings—which, in fact, may have been all there was—of love felt are no more than a blur in the distant background. Perhaps it is in search of how they felt—in search of the truths of love (or of the passions produced by the biological pressure to reproduce) that the narrator of *In Search of Lost Time* lingers for such absurd amounts of time on scenes and interpretations of forlorn or nasty or ludicrous love. One can remember that one played out a passion but the passion is past the point of no return, all that comes back is the memory: so much for the long reproductive years! Those were lively ones: joy, confusion, gratitude, shame, lust, pregnancy, uncertainty, protest, absurdity, Janis Joplin, war. Every day and all the way. "When should one live, if not in the time given to one?" We are never fully protected by sidewalks, window panes in vertical concrete slabs, supermarkets with their displays and checkout counters, rice cookers and immersion blenders, thumbtacks, electric cars, and Burger Kings from a clownish Zeus throwing thunderbolts from the clouds or from an insouciant gnome in a yellow slicker in the hills to the east rolling granite bowling balls at sandstone bowling pins.

In the classroom Rosie Consuela Hassan raises a question whose possible answer her students, like ponderous summer bears or quick nocturnal raccoons, are trying to track as if through a forest, across a swamp, and down to a flickering beach ground to grains. The task entails the application of text to matters at hand, much as a filmmaker sets images to music—or is it music to images? Latitudinal thinking discovers a cosmos comical in its coincidences, keeping its synchronies and its convergences in disguise or playing them out at deafening speed. Either way, for a moment at least, one history becomes indistinguishable from another. And here we have it: this beloved indeterminacy, rejection of efficient prose, the dismantling of representation, restless laughter in the stairwell as on the folding sea. Representatives disperse, scattering into "a world," to quote Anthony J. Cascardi, "that seems to be constructed around the *principle* of concealment." Representation hides in plain sight with names, the transparent cover-up, faint flickers of attention sent out as small thin clouds bloom against the sky. Sylvie Win Sarrault in the sandbox throws off her shoes and begins to shovel sand into a yellow sock at the park. Sylvie concentrates, watching the ever-changing correlation of motion, moments, and things; no critique intervenes; let's call this an inquiry into the conventions of the sock.

A CONE OF FRENCH FRIES is placed on the table in the basement bar—a black plastic wire-gridded cone-shaped basket lined with a sheet of crisp white paper, one corner rising defensively above one side of the basket to protect the thin-cut, salt- and rosemary-sprinkled fries from any fingers but Enrico's and mine. Fun is underrated; time throws its darts and they drop when they hit the wall. Why do so many people sneer at Chardonnay? "Few grape varieties elicit a knee-jerk reaction like Chardonnay," says an anonymous reviewer on the internet, "it's characterized as a heavy, opulent white wine, the antithesis to crisp, easy sippers like Sauvignon Blanc and Pinot Grigio." Fun is unintelligible—an alternative life making sense elsewhere projecting synchrony that the human senses are simply incapable of perceiving. There are revenants—the returning—they could be prodigals, could be ghosts, could just be people coming home from a trip, and there are *arrivants*—they show up for the first time with a surprising note at a turning point in a passage of music or a strange word in the fingers of a phrase. The moment of death—maybe it occurs as a quiet nullification, the cessation of specific event and of all eventuality, but maybe it's sublime, a moment of unsurpassable intensification, something akin to the shock of the real, or that shock itself.

Here under the sun I'll state that I'm telling lies voluntarily, though I hope inconspicuously. I'm lying not because I fear being caught in a crime or transgression, nor because of habitual truthlessness, nor out of malicious ennui or arbitrary spite, I'm lying in order to endow facts with the significance of events that should have happened but didn't or to deprive events of the significance that they shouldn't have. I'm lying in order to preserve facts as facts only, rescuing them for the perpetual present: cows eat grass, sun and air feed trees, the sum of the digits of all multiples of nine equal nine. Etc. Never underestimate etc.; the sum of all facts—it's the thin green film of chaos that separates the earth from the sky. As a girl, with a playing card secured to the front fender of her bike and protruding between the spokes so it repetitively snapped as the front wheel turned, Lola rode to the sound of hooves galloping over the ground; the resounding stud was a joker. If freedom existed it would do so in defiance of all attempts at organization, all representations of coherence.

If my skull were cracked open, would my mother be there, and, if she were, it would be as I remember her, right, and not as she actually was? The real question, though, is this: if my skull were cracked open, would *I* be there? I don't remember myself, only some contexts in which I was, and I was, in those contexts, unverifiably, so some doubt on this is warranted. But I'm not about to get my skull cracked (or crack it myself): I'll leave my skull intact and assume that there's a brain there; it prompts me now to reach for the crank on the north-facing window in front of me and open it to let the last of the light-bearing breeze brush the things on my desk: a vase of sunflowers, a jar of pens, scraps of paper, computer and keyboard, chapstick, a glass of wine, and on a short plastic stands an empty ostrich egg with a ¼ inch hole at one end. Poor egg! Poor shell! Poor Ostrich! Poor Yorick! The ostrich egg is a trinket, not a specimen, it's not even a souvenir; it's a thin strong upstanding ovoid bit of unoccupied matte mauve-gray matter.

Along comes a day—debilitating but not dispassionate—on which I'm beset by sloth and petulance, everything around me is either too trivial to tolerate or too irrelevant to bear or just too small to notice with anything other than irritation and self-pity. Forget the glory of the mote, the russet iota in a dead wet shell, the word, the shred, the single sun reflected in multiple windows on a hill facing east, the *radical particular* "materially opaque, interpretably complex, historically situated, and unsublatable to the whole." Here I am, wherever and whoever, in a moment that's fraught, frightening, enraging, saddening, and with what promises to be an unbearable future—why not exercise my ability to accuse, judge, and condemn—by name? What does it mean—to you, to me, to the many with names or names to come—that I'm writing this with a constantly unsettled sense of the urgency of this globally and locally devastated and devastating socio-political and climatological present moment and yet refer to its forces of destruction obliquely or not at all? We come to the elephant yard, paved and including scum and water in a shallow concrete pool and one elephant attached by one foot to a heavy chain bolted to the ground. The elephant is languidly or it might be mournfully or gloomily nuzzling a mound of hay with its trunk before seizing a scraggly wad and tossing it over its head on which dust and hay already hang like the veil of a stolid old woman demurely displaying her modesty, but a better comparison might be to the head of a pit bull that's been bullying rats in a barn. Every point of view depends on a point to view and it hovers somewhere beyond the viewer casting reality into the milieu of the moment, grimy or grim. I flounder around—I want to flounder around—in microcosms and macrocosms as Vivaldi's *The Four Seasons* begins with a flashback to a costume drama and ends mournfully in a cold house with *il cimento dell'armonia e dell'inventione*, "a contest between harmony and invention," undecided. Sentences no longer strengthened by strife disintegrate, a process Empedocles (that ancient Presocratic philosopher of two forces and the stuff of stuff) would have identified as the effect of love, which has the power, too, to dissipate virtue. There we see the reader, "she" for whom the poem is being written, who swoons as "you" yields to the raptures of what "he" calls the aesthetic, and now "we" will move a long way toward understanding the pathology governing literature. It involves a lot more masochism than you'd suppose. But there it is. And here we realize that we are getting off on personal subjection: we are getting fucked by the text. The disintegration of ego is going to continue.

It may be time now to pull out some boilerplate rhetoric and produce a phrase like "it's beyond the purview of the present work to . . ." or "it is not my task here to . . ." or "I won't here tax your attention or waste your time by . . . ," etc. But who am I to leave names stranded and deny them the truth of their isolated referentiality, the fact that they are mono-referential, their sheer obliquity? Each is the signifier for only one sole signified, both (to repeat Barrett Watten's eloquent characterization) "materially opaque, interpretably complex, historically situated, and unsublatable to the whole." It is precisely so as to embrace the *radical particular* in its adamantine specificity, its gritty quiddity, and its brash omnipresence, and to face its ultimate inaccessibility and hence its unrepresentability, that I began and will continue. I have considered the viability of that and am unsettling the cat on my lap so as to add a few words in language not meant to unveil anything, phrases free of obligations to glum interpretations of the moment. Humans have often thought their times were the worst—that's a truism that offers consolation of sorts: these are just bad times like others. But these are our times, this is our moment—why not attack its predators with at least verbal vengeance? Like that guy—remember that guy cursing from the curb ("motherfucking chrysanthemum ass turd swiper," "crypto-lipped mouse dick," etc.)? Sometimes storytelling catches on and catches up again: long ago, gather round, once, listen, says the storyteller, quickly, before the story gets too long, going on without untenable cause and without any particular end.

With far less authority and far less control than you might think, I continue with this work or lack of work, but I could deny responsibility for it by insisting that I'm only a proxy agent of the very language in which I'm writing, acting "of necessity" or under orders that I don't know I'm receiving. Things may rhyme but aren't identical, and "this," says a feminist scholar, forefingers writing glyphs in the air, "is to provide the wished-for surplus through which to resist being useful and being used." And my consciousness responds: I experience a small change, there are no true synonyms, the air itself is not indifferent to difference. All around lies the indirectness of an expanse, it's like an ocean between eyes and objects, if object they are, indifferent, without purpose, perfect, rising, replete, light-bound. *Limb gradient turnip truth* casts approbation just as leaves of some coastal tree cast shadows on the wall of a sunlit room while remaining only vaguely identifiable.

In order to sustain narrative and thus explanation, not to mention drama, historiography emphasizes the consequential, it operates in the language of "therefore," "thus," "because," "since," but often reality comprises things linked only apparently, their connections happenstantial and their significance always secondary. The language of agency, the language of forceful sentences and strong verbs depicting purportedly causative actors and forces charging the future—it works, but history itself is a slapdash affair. Herodotus records that a powerful personage once "called a town meeting" and there "revealed that the revered new civic statue had been recast from the bronze tub in which the citizens had vomited and pissed." No matter—as Richard Popkin in *The History of Skepticism* observes, "The only thing that seems to be clear and distinct and true is that what appears to somebody appears." From a neighborhood backyard Bruce the mixed breed Rottweiler barks at a low-flying helicopter churning overhead. With their barbarous sounds the heavy dog in his way and the helicopter pilot in hers are adding uncouth turbulence to the milieu and with that they are taking power. But you can't legitimately claim to be an automaker just because you display a fan belt, a tire, a crank shaft, and a steering wheel. It's sheer fantasy to suppose that humans could ever create a system of governance that would establish a benevolent society and bring about lasting good. Raking leaves off the sidewalk in front of a house in the city is a public display of the bourgeois housekeeping that preserves for the residents a kind of social fencing, an aesthetic façade behind which they lodge their privacy and, as far as Aquo Thomas Koury is concerned, the helicopter and the dog are irrelevancies: introspection, that strange and alluring in-turning of thought, furthers the fantasy that privacy ranges free of the very enclosures on which it depends.

TONY VAN HEUVEL, "the independent curator," feels toward a painting, he's holding off any possible narrative, he prefers the feeling or the exchange of feeling occasioned by his appearance before that of the painting; the relationship (such as it is, he thinks) is ambient, clear, and solitary, there's no emotional flooding, no aesthetic melodrama. Don't be fooled by whatever seemingly transparent sensibility emanates from any work of art including a piece of writing and be careful about attributing it to someone. It may seem that an individual has appeared, but how real is she or he or they (or you or I)? And how significant are individuals anyway—can we believe in their coherence, their lifelong continuity, do they have real efficacy as the shapers of history, societies, economies, cultures? If life could be (or be like) a work of art—or if art could transform ways of life—would we want it to be the work of some individual, no matter the degree of his or her or their genius? Don't for a minute think that I have control over words. Quite the contrary: they control me: I live between quotation marks. As Lola points out, people will never agree about art, even when they habitually and with little or no reflection can agree that others agree about some specific work of art. And anyway, according to whose aesthetic theories or standards or practices might art transform reality, John Coltrane's, Leonardo da Vinci's, Pablo Picasso's, Aretha Franklin's, Charles Dickens's, Hildegard von Bingen's, Leo Tolstoy's, Dorothea Lange's, Kazimir Severinovich Malevich's, Virginia Woolf's, Janis Joplin's, Johann Sebastian Bach's, Charlotte Brontë's? Well, life is insufficiently artistic. There should always be *something* attracting consciousness and inviting inspection, critique, judgment, and plan, though: causing attraction is inherent to *joie de vivre*. We say of Pippa Sidhu Petersdot that she is "full of herself," but what else should she be full of, to date it's herself that is the sole center of her known world and only source of her social power. In a basement room of the city archive, Lola is looking at a decades-old map of the underground utility pipes, sewage conduits, cables, and wires crisscrossing and intertwining under what used to be the bay shore's light industrial zone, an area she will characterize in her report as *now under gentrification* with the additional comment that all new construction there is underway over a *dangerously deteriorating infrastructure*. Lola adds, *Problem immediate—needs attention*; Lola adds a recommendation: *Give district a name so media will notice and make it news.*

Every statement is a composition; diverse elements are gathered, synchronized, and compressed into what may look and sound like a declarative statement but is, in fact, an extending speculation. It's a projection, mother to an alter ego. Definitely—you should nurture your private sensibility (your "inner life"). But don't stop there, as they say. Deploy it in social spaces ("public life"). Of course it won't affect large-scale systems—short-lived, small-scale utopian moments are the best you can hope for. But they're way worth the time and trouble! Imagination thinks, coming up with some odd scenario, a curious consequence, an interpretation of, say, the presence of an earwig exiting an Iceland poppy left by the ebbing tide—these may or may not give you confidence to trust appearances, including my own. Long lights cross into this room from the apartment building behind the house; only the shadow of the branches of a gaunt backyard tree intervenes between one built environment and another. Let's never forget the assertive power of grammar as it extends its sentences in myriad directions and entangles them in configurations that some see as chaotic, some as incomprehensible, a few as erotic. After all, the voluptuous curvatures as well as the alluring angles and enticing irregularities of the quotidian never completely vanish. Just as a carrot might consider a Kleenex box or a mermaid ponder a mustard jar or a cat negotiate a clamshell, so the east façade of the apartment building comes to an understanding with the morning sun. Every bit of perceptible stuff can be woven by its perceiver into that of some familiar object and thus he or she or they can observe an exciting world tilted at a comfortable pitch as a spider might in a breeze on a thread. For just a moment we can dive right out from under standardized time.

The air is a material substance crossed by an unidentified bird and favoring the senses which, as they savor the seemingly unlimited expanse in which to develop their knowledge and discover their ignorance, are packed to capacity. I cast my vote in favor of phenomenal reality and for phenomenal rationality too. You may be sprinkling pigment pepper on your eggs, but any good defense of the senses will insist that nonsense can't exist. From what then is this ego conjectured or concocted? Random juxtaposition might suffice: confectionary eroticism beginning with childhood afternoons on a swing in a schoolyard playground and ending with all this. Anxiety, ever convivial, reaches way back in history to include (as Marcus Tullius Cicero should know) "almost all the ancients, who said that nothing can be recognized or perceived or known; that the senses are constricted, the spirit weak, the course of life brief." After that the ancients must have called for leeks, turnips, olives, mutton, and wine.

At the moment—here and in this historical moment—the aesthetic will to soothe seems as strong as the aesthetic impulse to shock. Thinking back into historically earlier contexts, say that of the Homeric world long before Cicero's and always aware that such "thinking back" is sure to get things wrong, one could speculate that it was generally thought that, rather than subjective pleasure (or even just personal shelter and safety), the primary purpose of human goings on was to delight (or, at least, to entertain) the gods. People—in the logic of our disappearance, in our present rigidity, ricocheting off the external world, never safe from understanding—we are not producing the desired results. "There is no human being who having both passions and thoughts does not think in consequence of his passions—does not find images rising in his mind which soothe the passion with hope or sting it with dread"—so says George Eliot, who sees the conflict between reassurance and fear as inherent to the psychology of hope. Emphatically, Fiasco Bikash McBee declares, history has no angels! Embarrassed by his outburst, Fiasco Bikash McBee ups it: the only thing history looks at is shit—history itself is shit. I heard it all when I was on that dysfunctional jury, says Melissa Banjara Warren—the witnesses, the experts, the lawyers—it's all injustice, exploited and denied.

Okay, no one has total freedom, maybe no one has enough, not even enough for perceptual acumen—our so-called wiring protects us from things unseen, unfelt, unthought, unheard. The dancer hides all signs of exertion, the old die exhausted by their own banality. I get that artists can do a great job of dreaming up things that don't exist, says Lola, but that's my point, they don't exist. But what lies hidden in the depths of reason or whatever moves around along the edges of logic may provide reality with its gravity—that's what I'm thinking—and it may be all the more real for that, and it might give reality more freedom. I pause, a few seconds pass, I tap my coffee cup against Lola's and lean back in my chair to take a perspectival rest.

That could be a real midday downtown café scene not far from the Department of City Planning and the Environment housed in a squat building of shabby cement across the street from a fenced skateboard park. It could just as easily be a scene briefly presented in ways that seem to those who encounter it to lie within the realm of what's commonly understood as reality or very like it, rather than, say, a figment of hallucination or lies. It's realistic, not alien. But why not lies? History's great claim is that it will prove ultimate and can't be anything other than true. That may be, but it's not over yet. We travel in its orbit, not its track.

How come your name is Floka, asks Pilar Piana Fleye; Tasha doesn't know how to shake hands, she adds, after commanding the dog to do so and demonstrating obedience by lifting its right paw with her right hand. How determined are we? There's no immediate present accessible to human thought, thought is inevitably interceding, or maybe it's as one of the Presocratics said, the human senses are thought organs. Philip Kilmartin on his chair near the café lets his chin rest on this chest. Noor Bigelow notices, not the posture but the state of mind, some combination of dreaming and defeat, persistence and resignation, and, who knows, perhaps an element of performance, his paper cup is upright on his lap, and according to the sign propped against his chair he needs $210 by the end of the week / FOR RENT (his caption, Noor thinks). The human soul is located in the imagination, or so an author writes with a biographer's authority; fine, but where then is the imagination located? Sabrina Q. Wells is afraid to lose social reciprocity, afraid she'll fail to fulfill life's obligatory task which is (she believes) to forge attachments and keep them. Sabrina Q. Wells, casting aside the old metrics of established identity, comes into the café and takes a seat to play her part in the allegory of *Conviviality*. Mental restlessness is a device as well as a symptom, it has unrealized potential as it tracks the flight of a series of objects into escapist fantasies in the hope of fissuring dreams so as to let reality come through, the product of a different and differently powered imagination.

IN OUR PRESENT RIGIDITY, botanically speaking, with but mostly without fellow feeling, we encounter a building to bypass, a glitch requiring a work-around, a municipal barricade to crash, a law to break: Is our desire for consolation now greater than our desire for shock? The world of art is not a free autonomous zone. We are subjects within and of sequences of events whose sum total is establishing a new trajectory and a new structure of existential being. Are we before a tribunal or serving on it? "This tribunal is nothing less than . . . ," "this tribunal is nothing more than . . ."—what? I intend it to provide grounds for another day though I can't summon up much optimism about human perceptual acumen and intelligence nor about human willingness to use them. But Dude, Dudessa, Dudette, let's go with the happenstantial and follow the noise of our toes; even the dogs on their leashes have aspirations.

Stories get told (or, more frequently, passed along) for the sake of a common, shared life—a culture. Stories get told to convey new information or to resituate things with additions, corrections, new perspectives, negations. As for negation and even negativity itself, they always carry subjacent disappointment strong enough to be indistinguishable from anger, but what's ultimately going on as stories evolve is a battle over rationalism, with joy lying on the field. There it is—joy, whose task is to make desire possible. There are no conclusions; stuff just generates suggestions, making an appeal to our capacity to appreciate contradictions and our ability, though exercised only weakly and sporadically, to resist the summons to wish-fulfillment. What, after all, is the story of an upholstered armchair, a tea bag, rain? Each is lodged in a politics not of its own making.

FIVE

Matter never leaves meaning untouched.

JAMES I. PORTER

TO A NAME, more or less barred from detours—some particular you or he or she or I—what can we add? Humans, memories of love and fucking (the latter of which is carried out under the auspices of love in the excellence of banal darkness)—each of us are the product of a fuck. Names, on the other hand—names and, if and when they appear, characters—leap from the imagination. Zander Blue Dallas, Reggie Clara Toss, Aquo Thomas Koury—and in better works Dorothea Brooke, Janie Mae Crawford, Charles Swann—these aren't predicates (characteristics, characterizations). May 1—International Workers Day; it's easy these days to get a sense of a seemingly sudden dehumanizing unreality. Cement hardens as the sun descends behind the commercial buildings on Angle Avenue; a red and white sign on a sandwich board stands at the Flutter and Angle crosswalk: "Sidewalk Closed." It occasionally seems that we still live haphazardly according to the seasons: no matter how great the distance is between us and the ancient first days of May, for example, on which demands for dance were made, here and there groups of schoolchildren today skip or pommel around a pole, interlacing colored streamers, which, now already tattered, flutter in the fog—the seasons: each a playing time and field with players.

Even before the infant can crawl, he or she discovers borders, brinks, edges, sides, and then, once he or she is on the move, others: friends, enemies, comrades, playmates, competitors, lovers. With these, with their respective logics of adjacent things, a person is living a life, its moments variously strung. Is this how we discover time, retrospectively, as an accumulation of moments, or do we discover it anticipatorily by feeling about for moments ahead? Moments? The accretion of stuff, rather, people, places, activities, and things—the makings of moments at eventful intersections: glowing ochre concavities pocking a ledge of sandstone, five motorcyclists threading traffic on a highway, a plover's nest at the edge of a picnic site near the city shore line, Micah Andre Blake beside me in the stands at the first gymkhana of the spring in, he says (gesturing toward his flipflops and shorts), the "wrong clothes," "and you think these are the right ones?" Noor asks (she points to her sandals, she's perpetually irritable), "just don't get stepped on."

It should be easy to keep going and even to stay lively, there's always a lot to do and there's reality everywhere, but all speculative propositions, all statements of intention, all promises, all narrative "realisms," are absurd given the narrow scope of humanity's temporal consciousness, its fixedly short-term imagination. Our anticipations are for the all but immediate. Time is lost not only because of inattention or forgetfulness but also by virtue of failed expectation and the failure of expectations. But we lose time, too, simply because of the limits of the future—or because the future doesn't (by definition) exist at all. It's not always our fault that we lose.

Life propels itself, moving to move, engaged in pure motion. Fragments of narrative are scattered about, undistributed, willy-nilly, indeterminate; the assemblage exists but unintentionally; it depicts nothing, lacks pattern or design though we can hope that it will produce effects. However does one indefatigably exercise skepticism without falling victim to laughter? To quote Lola: The more a person learns, the sharper her wit. Original thought—it's a matter of infinite regress, the memory of everything. Instead of the link-by-link associative formation typical of montage we come face-to-face with disparate multicontextual and polysemous matter with no discernible purport—a disarrangement, maybe even a derangement, judged to be a manifestation of nonsense or even madness, weakening if not entirely destroying the mechanisms customarily used for sense-making. But all's not lost: the shaping power of memory may serve to counter the chaos, though in doing so it inflates one with self-aggrandizing nostalgia, making an almost irresistibly flattering appeal to one's subjectivity, singling one out as a secret but transcendent center of experience.

As Nietzsche said, "There are no isolated judgments!" We very well might experience subjectivity as an interior presence, but it's not a single one. As for personality—how variably it plays about when others are around and even as occasional (contextual) disappointments flash. Julia Xanthe Jones is an artist only for the sake of Art, says Tony van Heuvel, subsuming Jones's amorphous works into a category for which his best definition is *You know it when you see it*. You think art is just a ball thrown into the air until it falls so we can kick it down the road to give us aesthetic distance?

The dictionary is a grand and truthful masterpiece even when it's responsible for the lesser works we call autobiographies. Can one characterize mortality as the inescapable condition of separability, dividing nonexistence from existence, individual particular from the collective (and collecting) phenomenal world? We can't prevent the meaning structures of our contexts from total breakdown. Happily, in less time than it takes to bake a potato, the dictionary stirs up another tumult of language with its loudest vowels and most raucous consonants sending waves of polysemy rolling through even the most quotidian, banal, pedestrian, and seemingly inconsequential of situations. And so I mock my vanity and even my presence with its illusory faces and fantasy ideals, as if my mockery could assert my superiority over them.

I may sometimes sound like a modern pop singer here but she will not demand that the public be interested in my personal condition, unlike those individuals who force their personality into their poetry—poetry is not for my concealed autobiography any more than it's for hers or for yours. Tragedy requires heroic tones, comedy the sounds of everyday life, as federal officers sneak about, seizing children who have taken off their shoes to run barefoot in the playground sand, rounding them up, loading them into a bus and handing them over to a private-public partnership for sorting, reshoeing, and release to the custody of year-round boarding schools for shearing and education: preparation for bleating and rage. "The body aches," Maria Stepanova writes, "it itches, it is full of fear, it tries and fails to forget itself, but the beholding eye moves freely and without haste, as if it were the air itself with its unlimited reserves of time." But we are really just watching blue marks on a grid: racism, bay leaves, bed sheets, unemployment, bruised elbows, hypochondria, yard sales, droughts, rice cookers, email messages, burn-out, mental health crises, corporatized education and for-profit prisons, melting glaciers, toothpaste, pandemics, pine trees, salt, white vernal clouds, hand cream, peanut butter, tents, ATMs, gender violence, turnpikes, robins, mass shootings, home repairs, indexes and lists and inventories. It's a given world, but whether it's proffered as a gift or as a joke or as a trick to fool us is hard to determine, and what or who would do the proffering in the first (or in any) case? It's just one thing after another, without explanation or justification and without much definition. As for Materia Tamayo-Cole, the detective—she'll just opt for what Charles Altieri calls "the pleasure of embracing appearances."

WHAT GAMES THEY PLAY in the supermarket arena! Floka parks her cart to one side in the wide space between the onions and the tiered display of tomatoes and avocadoes to ponder the aesthetics of the produce display, the bouquets of curled bananas, the carefully outspread carrots, tops removed and fanned between untopped beets to the right and rutabagas to the left, yellow onions in a stable heap beside white onions on one side and red onions on the other with shallots and heads of garlic in baskets leaning against the onions and slightly tipped in her direction: a controlled abundance, surreptitiously spotlit. This is ideology in performance before ranging shoppers, a demonstration of plenitude, perfection, and (for those who can pay for them) availability; ideology as good as captions it: *National Bounty*, *Nature's Wealth*, or *Life's Riches*, embedded in melancholy, a growing blur of smudges and marks depicting something indecipherable, obscure, and forestalling interpretation. What's there to see? One looks at a photograph in anticipation of what lurks behind or below its surface, the very thing it can't show: animation, action, personality, life. Major theorists of photography (Eduardo Cadava, Walter Benjamin, Roland

Barthes, and Jérôme Thélot among them) consider a photograph to be a site of death—"cadaver is the other name of photography," as Jérôme Thélot puts it—but four pages before quoting that comment of Thélot's, Cadava suggests something quite different by proposing an affinity between photography and motherhood: "mothers are always another name for photography—mothers and photography are both means of reproduction." Humans put their hands everywhere—Floka Claire Gregory adds two red onions to the items in her cart and pushes it into the aisle between berries imported from Mexico in plastic "clam shell" containers and piles of citrus fruit, the oranges jubilant, the tangelos belligerent, the grapefruits paunchy.

"There were things needing to be acknowledged that were outside the scope of what could be represented and indeed that the conventions of representation served to conceal"—this is Anthony J. Cascardi summarizing the challenge that Francisco de Goya faced as he set about depicting things of his time in the contexts of the time. Appearing as a name in, say, a book provides the named with a textual life, which, somewhat like the life of a being that appears in a photograph, is a past life arriving now from the dead zone that is the full context in which that being lived, except that a name in a text may have no other being than that provided by the letters of the name, viz. Lola, Tina Madhurmita Skye, Enrico Wren Roberts, Cyrus Ratad, Milly Margaret Willis, Tamarind Magee, and I. We assign names to persons to facilitate their discontinuity; their names produce their appearances and their names allow them to disappear. Or, to put that another way: a name is a machine of repetition, facilitating absence just as much as it summons appearance. As for I—I can be dead but still writing. Voilà: you could interpret this as another of the machinations of capitalism as it carries out the monetization of eros and the erosion of hours: "part of the history of absence." And think of all the things—new or surprising—that are underway as I write: self-driving cars, AI, socio-political polarization and first world governmental corruption and dysfunctionality, privately-owned spacecraft, massive worldwide reduction in biomass of flying insects, murder by cops. As for "this tribunal"—under what auspices does it have authority? Lola saddles Night on a weekend morning, Freya Cyprian Slight walks up the three cement stairs to the library, Leo X. Lee plays scales in his garage.

"The entire world entered the posthistorical phase when [. . .] it lost its faith that history could be overcome." What Boris Groys is referring to is human history or, more pointedly, a history of human ambition, greed, injustice, and cruelty—conscious human viciousness. But Groys is referring to something else, too, something entirely different and counter to history as one of human atrocities: history not as a record of what's happened but, rather, history as a force that "strives toward consummation." History doesn't achieve consummation (whatever Groys or his translator means by that term), history strives toward it. "And when history no longer strives toward consummation, it disappears, ceases to be history, stagnates." The point here is that the history humans produce is vicious, but this very history is produced in the course of a quest for utopia: humans seek utopia in order to put an end to their cruelty and they are cruel in their pursuit of it. I think I prefer coincidence to causation in real life, Samantha Jane Jenkins says to Jovanna Tupac Milton as she rings up the sale of the book Jovanna Milton is buying, but detective novels can be great. Jovanna Tupac Milton wants to find constructive principles in *irrational* thought, a logic *in* (not *of*) unreason, she wants to intensify a feeling for life (her feeling, our feeling) by exposing the inevitability of reason's loss of command, the loss even of its possibility. Especially, Jovanna Milton says as she passes her credit card to Samantha, when the detective and his family eat really good food. Consciousness, even if only as a sorting of sensations, exists prior to reason, but without reason consciousness would be immobilized, static, incapacitated. What then, in this state of maximal unfreedom, would be subject to remembering? We come to know ourselves imaginatively rather than rationally, however, utilizing the fictions we declare, founded on histories we concoct to verify the stories and the characters we think we are or want to be. To achieve this, and it's no small thing and requires the complicity of others, we have to start early and often and know when to lie. As Adorno says, "[W]hat once seemed to be reality emigrates into imagination, where it survives by becoming conscious of its own unreality."

I realize that I should try beginning yet again, interpreting, but interpreting what—interpretation? It's perpetually disturbed, or both of them are: the beginning and the interpreting. And on what grounds are either possible, on what grounds is possibility possible? There are nothing but material grounds; all around us matter exercises its erotic attraction—to that even the dead respond as their atoms and molecules shift, disperse, dissolve. If we take this proposition seriously, it follows that the dead don't—or don't necessarily—stop. That said, all question of progress is moot. The second hand on the analog clock with hypnotic regularity takes its tiny jump from spot to spot and beguiles one into forgetting time.

A successful performance of realism must look and sound like the real thing: it must fully resemble what our observations, education, and social milieu have led us to believe reality *is*. To engage with fiction (literary or cinematic)—to engage through enjoyment or curiosity or out of scholarly interest, etc.—entails the adoption of certitude, the famous or infamous willing suspension of disbelief. In effect, meanwhile, realism may have as much scope as reality, though they include different things. Meaning casts music, sense propels sound. Turn up the music! Here's the thing (Cyrus Ratad is free of doubt), here's the thing (he continues, finger pointing, not like the Lenin we see in statues but with elbow bent and arm only chest high), you live in Lalaland, not in the real world. And (I think) you do? Because (he wags his finger and lowers his arm)—put it like this: I have taught myself to ignore my feelings. The technocratic takeover of reality and the transformation of reality into a battleground—it would indeed be deafening, it already is—even realism would be gone from reality.

Labor white plight stick of pencil ink and sponge in the mug of rules: this is full of semantic potential but what comes of it depends on the local circumstances, how the words are arrayed, the facts functioning, what those bent on utilizing, seizing, appropriating, monetizing, weaponizing, and exploiting do next. *Lagging plastic,* it says, or *rising bread pamphlet and wet sleeve.* Through no fault of its own, it's nonsense. But, making a return, realism could sweep all of this away and who could blame it, even if it were sometimes wrong? The names of birds, says Tamarind Magee—robin, finch, pigeon . . . (*every*-one knows robins and pigeons—*Ob*-viously, says Pilar Piana Lye) . . . give us birds to see. Pilar is certain but not wrong; there are some propositions that, as Wittgenstein puts it, "lie apart from the route travelled by enquiry." They provoke feeling, not emotion but an a priori sense of something, an initial and immediate intuitive comprehension. It can be the shelf of a store and a wind turbine too—the whole elastic, so to speak—generating platitudes ("to entertain is to be entertained," "to appreciate is to gain in appreciation," and the like). There is more to where there is less than you might think—*Ob*-viously, as Pilar would say.

The produce market on Flats Ave has fresh English peas again, and Enrico Wren Roberts is adding some—podded and rinsed—to the leek risotto he's making; a chunk of Parmesan and a flat grater are already on the table, the green salad is lightly dressed, and six sea scallops, patted dry and sprinkled with black pepper, are on a plate ready to sear in butter as soon as the skillet's hot. Reggie Clara Toss looks up from the table where she's been sewing and asks, "What's for dinner?" and when in response to his answer she says "Amazing," Enrico lifts his wooden spoon and waves it like a baton, conducting her into rising from her chair and doing a plié. The violin arches, the quotidian is meaningless, somewhere in fields cows rest, and syllogistic logic comes up blank. For Enlightenment philosophers (Kant is the one most often cited in this context), ethics was to "rest on rational grounds" and "have universal scope," as the art historian/philosopher Anthony J. Cascardi puts it. On the other hand, for Francisco de Goya, about whom Cascardi is writing, "questions of ethics are inseparable from affect, which is to say," Cascardi continues, "both that they communicate by appeal to the emotions and also that they regard the emotions as integral to ethical life." The trick here is to regard the quotidian as an instrument and not just a theater for ethical life. Admittedly, limits to personal agency are set by the number of available options for action but also by the purported agent's uncoordinated desires and incommensurate motives which, without one's full knowledge, prompt one to act as one does. As an agent, one is poorly defined. Antonia Alice Martin, Max Marie Ritter, Cornelia Katrina Cabanatuan, Ulysses Theo Upton, Bonnie Rose Roberts—they carry on by dint of mobility and are all but invisible (like wind in still, dishonest air).

BOTH DISCORD AND HARMONY PREVAIL in the quotidian cosmos of stuff: can opener; Knudsen's non-fat cottage cheese; Paper Mate Sharpwriter #2 pencil; size 7½ Baflinger Reine Schurwolle slippers; emery board; packet of 140 Post-it flags (languettes, banderitas); square, striped box of Signature Select tissues; dust bunny in corner; cat on bed; and so on—stuff for those who love the incontestable necessities and the inessential deadwood, extraneous, superfluous, merely handy. But let's accord some justice to the useless and so-called trivial and grant some efficacy to the things that seem hardly worth noticing. Let's take a breath. Here lies the given world with its many simultaneities, rich with amiability as well as strife, stress, and discord. But justice—justice for field guides and for dirt, ferns, succulents, sands? Anaximander's variously interpreted comment, recorded by Simplicius one thousand years after Anaximander's time and based on the only extant fragment of his writings, puts it this way: "The source of coming-to-be for existing things is that into which destruction, too, happens '*according to necessity; for they pay penalty and retribution to each other for their injustice according to the assessment of Time,*' . . ." The classicists Kirk, Raven, and Schofield provide this with a plausible interpretation: "the prevalence of one substance at the expense of its contrary is 'injustice,' and a reaction takes place through the infliction of punishment by the restoration of equality—of more than equality, since the wrong-doer is deprived of part of his original substance, too," and less than a page further they add, "The idea of a time-limit is appropriate: the injustice of summer has to be made good within the roughly equal period of winter, that of night during the period of day, and so on . . . ; Time makes the assessment to meet the particular case." But in the short term, the only term humans seem to comprehend, what do we get—a crone crooning ballads to a diamondback rattler on a stool, a mathematician with an ivory spoon savoring slices of grapefruit sprinkled with sugar, a jazz band performing in a basket under a hot air balloon over the financial district, a collection of ornately framed ads for cat food displayed on the wall behind a bowling alley bar. Time is not without wit, but a crow born as a crow will die as a crow.

Person, group, neighborhood, landscape—each has its ways, automatically maintained. "My habits have their home territory," Tony van Heuvel says, aimlessly giving the cork beer coaster a counter-clockwise quarter turn, "far from Certitude; it's more like Confusion, but that's better than Rigidity." This is allegorical thinking, something impossible without a penchant for picturing—"explaining the facts of the world in terms of the things of the world," Byron D. O'Farrell adds. Zander Blue Dallas laughs; "There was no first decision," he says, "though maybe there was a first problem. Or a first perception of a problem." Jubilantly Byron D. O'Farrell continues: "The product of strife or time or water or justice or fire or freedom or chaos—or perhaps the first problem was that of absurdity." Off in a crowd of pedestrians crisscrossing the late afternoon shadows softening the cement, Placo Paris Wang says something to Materia Tamayo-Cole, something about two tents or two dents.

Losses are real in the phenomenal world where dogs and cats, bread and butter, celery and peanut butter, ice cream and cake, apple pie and automobiles, roots and branches get paired, by association if not always of necessity, though the pairings often enough feel fixed if not inescapable. And since meaning accrues in increments, each detail can only signify somewhat and every detail ultimately gets subsumed (though not obliterated). And always there's the quivering potential for new pairings, both reproductive and productive: AI and jelly, granite and the ace of spades, athlete and cutlery, ballgown and persimmon, emerald and skillet. Many things converge at (or with) names to form a single (and, let's not forget, singular) congregation. Meanwhile, a single language in being shared becomes many. Myriad thoughts get propelled by grammar gears. The comedy of coupling plots continues on, with "jarring juxtapositions and miscommunication," "mighty patches of incoherence," "layered, inconsistent, and jumbled ontologies"—anything might crop out or up.

Ghosts hate to be bothered, and so we are tossed in and out of dreams patched together from the "hours, days, months" that John Donne called the "rags of time." Dreams lie in the dark like banners tattered by the sun, signals from a zero-point in phenomenal space. It seems that imaginative fulfillment is impossible, perhaps precisely because it's the stuff of mortality and, like everything mortal, it's timed. But ultimately and primordially, space and time are not only inseparable but the same, maintaining the cosmos, the infinite finitude keeping things grounded, holding in the ghosts. And with similar reciprocity, though perhaps on a vastly smaller scale, every state of knowledge is a state of feeling and with every feeling we encounter knowledge along with concomitant affective and epistemological doubt. It's not the task of reasoning to reason us out of feeling; intellect without sensibility is not what it takes to be rational. So what are these ghosts? Or, rather, how is it that they are as impersonal as beauty while nonetheless being far from indifferent? Beauty is too stodgy, it can't cope with the plethora of appearances, it can't cope with all that's presented as the present (say, dead bodies under rubble, reptilian lava curling around cars, a broken bicycle below a cliff, a hospital in flames), it can only tear it narcissistically from time in the name of art or perhaps in the name of justice, shame, social critique, grief, virtue. Or whatever. Imagine a painting, its primary structuring clear: it's considerably higher than wide. Or let it be a doorway into a room—the evidence suggests that it's early morning but it might be late afternoon, the hour depends on the actual use of it, pinot noir poured into the glass of evening, a building manager's broom at 8:15 a.m. swishing across a band of sunlight zigzagging up the short flight of stairs from the sidewalk to the front door. Somewhere along an uninteresting inland intercity highway, the present tense has surreptitiously slipped into the past with a spectral peach tree, the widespread glow of wild mustard, a small collapsing wooden shed. Happily, there's no grammatical confusion, that perpetrator of fear.

If only I wrote quickly, fashioning phrases, forming sentences, moving words, with thoughts in a frenzy, matter gyrating, matters at hand: spoons and broken trade agreements and gravel and google searches and toddlers at play and identity theft and deer droppings on an urban path and the recovery of a stolen Vermeer. Everything would accrue the coherence imposed by hurry and a restricted amount of time, a time of mind in an epistemological mood catalyzed by touch typing expertise and an aphoristic method, each scrap or shard or splinter or shred drawn into a wild and subversive haven for a festival of misunderstandings. Onto the page, across the screen, into the mind there might appear a tall pine tree captured in a red dress—why not? Stars on a trip, boys baking pies, flamboyant rain, textual seas. I could write about anything; knowledge might be sporadic, intermittent, cast in fragments, each "fierce, declarative and self-cancelling, not edging toward the truth of consciousness step by qualified step." *Carpe diem*—apples and atheists are on parade. Pumping a playground swing with sedentary verve and situated understanding, Pilar Piana Lye defies gravity even as she bends and draws and bends it again to form something like a gravitational cocoon around her, a hemisphere through which, back and forth, she curls and rides. Pilar goes as high as she can until she tires and gravity subsides. Surely there's room for philosophical skepticism in fantasy, making a mess of the rule-abiding drama of cause and effect. The alphabet may indeed invite play (A is for Artichoke, Z is for Zilch, etc.), but the role it plays is like that of an MC or DJ, calling up a strange assortment of presentations. As Sextus Empiricus puts it, "We use the term 'are' for the term 'appear.'" Just check out the grammar school playgrounds at recess time on a Friday in May. Samantha Jane Jenkins does so as she walks north on Mount Foot Avenue, one step at a time—a game in which she too defies gravity in a sequence of plays—a material sequence, a model of logic, a matter of course. If all logic is sequential, it's only because matter is in step with time.

There are things I'm choosing to know and things I'm definitely choosing not to know, knowledge I'm seeking or am turning away from. But inevitably thinking wanders off, drawn perhaps by beauty (which knows nothing at all) or love (whose attractions are scarcely epistemological). The comedy of modes moves on. The turning shadow of a tree, the turning of the tuning peg on a guitar, the incoming roll of quasi-white clouds, the slowly moving wheels of a gravel truck climbing a hill, the churning legs of dogs in the park: there is no place for missing limbs in an anatomical study of temporal display. When asked about acting, the actor says that the act is nearly impossible, the outcome unknown every time, the physical risks inescapable, the social residues ineradicable—"for better *and* worse," adds the actor.

"The impossible is made possible in context." For this to be true, a context has to be made possible. It's not by chance that I pull a copy of *Jacques le fataliste* from the bookshelf—I go to the bookshelf precisely for the purpose of looking into the book. "If you aren't paying attention, it's either because you aren't thinking about anything at all or because you are thinking about something other than what's in front of you"—this, more or less, is the sentence that catches my eye (as if it were a wren on a rock) when at random I open the book. It's Jacques who's speaking: *Get back in context*—that's what he's saying—or *Get yourself into my context*. The trouble with elevating the power of reason to a preeminent position and giving it ultimate authority is that it is always *someone*'s reason. But why this obsessive thinking about thinking, the inner silence of language?

MY LAP IS CLEAR. But that's not true: the cat jumps off my lap and with that I open my notebook on it, black jeans overlapped by the gnarled, mottled wool of a drooping sweater. Lying is only one of the many devices to which writers stoop (or rise like a ballet dancer *en jeté*). You might ask to what purpose the writer lies or disorders his, her, or their phrases, or deflates an idea, or contradicts their, her, or his own propositions, or comes to no conclusion. You might ask my name. Come on—use your imagination. To get you started I'll say that it's neither Teresa Lisa Tan nor Guillermo Jack Pelliet nor Natalia Lakshmi Nelson nor Travis Butch, and with that I've reached an autobiographical limit beyond which I won't go.

It continues to astonish me that things of the phenomenal world show themselves—but of course that's precisely what they do: appear! Voilà—and with that, as they make themselves present, we launch into interpretation, judgment; we make adjustments to our cognition. And we come up with names. But hasn't it been proven, meanwhile, that *names* can prompt *things*? What is this—a pudding? It's just the latest, but far from the last, thing to appear, and it might not be a pudding but, rather, something like a pudding: a mound in a dish, a dune in a bowl—finely swirled sand, or mud. A simile is like the happy smile with which Narcissus comes face to face with his beautiful self at a woodland pool.

Now past, what was a tableau is now an event, though only minor, momentary, and one of many. You can't untell a tale, you can't undream a dream; even forgetfulness remains incomplete. What might the future bring, beyond evidence, that is, that something happened or, at least, existed? And after that—fingers on lips, the body for pleasure, beautiful nonchalance, ginger snaps and chocolate ice cream, or myriad things far worse which we'd experience with fear, sadness, or horror. With every passing moment the scenario from which we begin our long departure into the future changes, each with its own materials for consumption, few of which we refuse.

Enrico Wren Roberts holds an egg in his hand; suddenly he fully recognizes what it is. I won't say he *realizes* what it is—the egg carries out its own realization; it sits in his hand being real and he's afraid of it, his fingers are too small for it, his thumbnail looks at him, timorous as a child or a mouse. Is *nausea* really the right term for what Antoine Roquentin experiences when he's face to face with the impervious quiddity (one might even say the perverse actuality) of physical things; wouldn't *revulsion* be the better term? Sartre, of course, would know, but Jean-Paul Sartre was a ponderous thinker, not a graceful one. Roquentin doesn't wretch, doesn't vomit. Enrico Wren Roberts is erecting a barrier between himself and the egg in his hand. He cracks the egg into a skillet and turns the flame down to prevent the butter under the egg from spattering onto the stove top; his irritability increases, strengthens, then it branches. Without conceptual constructs—without categories and the practicalities they sustain—there'd just be us, or rather you, me, Enrico Wren Roberts, and things—a melee, madness, absolute alienation, a plethora of disjunct particulars stripped of association, unlinked—a universe of estranging plenitude. We'd have no way to think about it.

My school is a perfect system, Pilar Piana Lye says to her grandmother; every Monday my teacher (Pilar says it precisely) *delegates tasks* and this week I'm in charge of setting out the morning snack, they rotate. The long-term repetitive present tense of the system is reassuring: to be dependable is a sure sign to Pilar Piana Lye that what's happening is logical, grammatical. And she's not wrong: such and such is the way we do things as we engage in recurrent acts of verification. With just a few words, Pilar Piana Lye is produced and here, too, is Milly Margaret Willis, timely, she thinks, when with unflappable sincerity Pilar lays out the snacks: cauliflower crackers (gluten-free), strawberries (rinsed), and half-pints of milk (already open and each flaunting a biodegradable straw). So much for narrative action, social observations, and doing literary justice to the facts. If a sentence makes sense, then other things do—public transportation, jokes, kickball, history. A work of art is always social and always necessarily a product of its epoch but other epochs (and other places) enter into its making as forces, influences, and materials and also as outcomes and alternatives—futures.

We encounter urban neighborhoods, weary city parks, classrooms, the impatient bay swept into fog, the reading room of a public library, the subterranean system of pipes and wires threading through the dark, all thick with impassible contradictions; we accept or even embrace them with melancholy. Impossibility guarantees our right to melancholy. But I'm no lyric melancholic. There's no Freudian melancholy here, by the way, though things must be different in German. Blondie Jane Carter, hunched under a torn, overstuffed laundry bag and trying to manipulate a stroller heaped wide with belongings including a blue tarp and a doll off a crowded bus, shrieks at someone—real or imaginary—on the bus behind her as she gets her stuff down. Let's call her mood *grungy melancholy*: Blondie Jane Carter—solid, sullen, and undefeated. Still, melancholy is the weakest form of affirmation, an exhausted form of vitality.

We've long been abroad in the fields of unverifiable propositions—territory, some would say, through which we can only *feel* our way. Individually and collectively, beings are going about their business interpreting appearances, dreams, ideas, and every interpretation complicates what appears. Most of the time for humans it's in language that interpretations make their appearance—language, the medium of complication, sensing appearances, spinning concepts like "the spider that crouches, forever silent, listening to the gay chirping of autumn insects," but never silent, so not like the spider, more like white noise trying to obliterate pain. Our thinking is hardly tidy, it's a jumble of letters on a Mobius strip, a phonic blur on Flats Ave, a shift of phrases as the breakfast menu is replaced by the menu for lunch. Someone means *bells* when somebody says *helicopter*, *winner* when someone says *nudge*. Just for the pure pleasure of quotation, let's call this "somebody whose voice everyone says appears to be standing still on one pitch then another." But concepts aren't mere distractions; the matter versus metaphysics dispute is as inane as the form versus content distinction. Behold the thousandth bold uncertainty: a marigold! Or maybe a zinnia?

WHAT IS THIS, then, a work of art placing phenomena before us, me as much as you—or anyone? Words—*a dog!*—and we see one. Every linguistic construct—every turn of phrase—involves an artistic element, even if it's not intentionally or properly presented as a work of art. And we are deceived; the language may be a material fact, but a "roaring dell, o'erwooded, narrow, deep, / And only speckled by the mid-day sun"? It's dubious that we're perceiving anything more than the shaken shadow of a perforated scene inviting our presence. But of course the sun casts contradictions: sunlight is an aid to appearance. Or is it just that a phrase, as an aid to prophecy, is self-fulfilling?

Humans like to make stuff. I suppose we could ascribe this to an underlying impulse to generate appearances—to the artistic impulse, say, or the need to make (up) a world—but making stuff seems to be what the busy world, producing and reproducing, does all on its own. Applying the term *art* to this activity is little more than granting it a seal of approval from culture monitors and monumentalizers. *The Rape* (or, more properly, the *Abduction*) *of the Sabine Women*: I suppose we could consider Livy's account of it and perhaps also Rubens's and Poussin's paintings of it, as monuments to gender, celebrating (if that's the right word) a landmark event in the struggle for human reproduction (or the male right to it). What would Rome be without those abductees? Making stuff has survival value—take nest-building, hive-building, web-building, etc., not to mention roads, wheels, huts, houses, and then cars, rockets, robots, and rubber bands. Alas, as Diderot pointed out long ago, "The person who makes our prosperity is condemned to die in poverty." Every monument is an irritable allegory, reaching at considerable expense for a story—*the* story, with plot and protagonist, crisis, blood, noise, and nudity. We're more than halfway through spring and we're summoned by an unarticulated thought to what we hope will be a satisfying event, as a horse might be to the far end of a field by the sound of a call and rattling oats in a bucket or as a bee might be to flowering sage, to discover the unconscious wish and "the phantasy in which this wish is embedded." So let's not forget war: every dead soldier honored as a hero here was the protagonist in an inevitable tragedy. Andre Micah Blake on the rodeo grounds turns to Aquo Thomas Koury and explains the stolid cloverleaf configuration in the arena while astride their horses outside the ring the contestants mill about or scrutinize the barrels and the course. This too is part of the memorial or of the day devoted to it, a mobilized festive competitive performance that, like immobile somber statues, monumentalizes what's commonly held to be the public's sense of brotherhood and battle—does it satisfy some self-perpetuating civic need without imposing the implacability of a massive but vague monument on the landscape—an embodiment of a national paradox, an imperious riddle? Well, questions like these are just propositions in disguise. The Sphinx did not have anyone's well-being in mind.

SIX

We are all of us imaginative in some form or other,
for images are the brood of desire.

GEORGE ELIOT

THINGS ARE MOVING as they do in everyday life, or, rather, in this one, abrupt, struggling, self-important, dehumanized, crazed, dying—and expensive, but money's a matter of structure rather than style. Tom Victor Kraft steps into the crosswalk ("zehbra" they call it in Russia, for some reason I think this to myself as I watch him) and he walks (saunters, struts—does anyone say *shashays* anymore?) across the busy (but sub-eventful) street, causing cars (the fenders of a red one look like enameled fingernails) to slow or halt as he leaves behind other pedestrians (the rest of us) obeying the red light. There you have it: two power structures, at odds in theory, but Tom Victor Kraft knows the odds. The light turns green and Tom Victor Kraft turns back and walks into the crosswalk again: *pissing thug fuckers, slime baby birth idiots, NOW you see me!* And now he stalks back to the sidewalk and down the street: another mini-drama, another confession. Much depends on a sentence, but more depends on its position, on the wielding of the power of the rules and the brandishing of the power of the unruly. Tom Victor Kraft turns right and disappears down Ashen Avenue ending the presence not of a moment of being but of a being at a moment—a being bearing (and baring) being: clever but not clever enough. The neighborhood has too many centers; it's hard to know what *that* prompts what *this*; intimations produce the neighborhood feel (as if wafting from some ancient quarry), but ramifications are hard to follow and judgments are just inventions. Each appearance announces a particularity, but too often we miss or ignore it or we gloss over it, replacing the individuated *that* with a conceptual *kind* or *kind of* or an exhaustive, casual, dismissive *whatever*.

How delicious absurdity once seemed—present, resonant, and full. Now absurdity is withered—dulled. By sadness? Well, if we can't feel happiness, at least we can mime it. I can do that, certainly: even until recently, I thought that life in all its plenitude and power was full of merriment, joy, beauties, vagaries, wonders—a panoply of distributed and redistributed realities, all more than merely apparent. Don't I still? And shouldn't I, at least for all practical purposes? How strange—I'm actually thinking this merrily, picking up the sounds of a squirrel somewhere in the sun outside the open windows of the gallery, moved by its rhythmic vigorous chattering—scolding? defiant? warning? Triumphant! The squirrel's sudden silence is definitive; now: a moment (long enough) of well-being. Tony van Heuvel swirls the spot of red light from his laser pointer around the bottom right corner of the painting before us: here in this area the whole narrative we saw depicted in the painting comes to nothing, doesn't even leave a mark—a viewer would only see it if they came to the painting looking for nothing. Where will I be ten, twenty, ninety years from now—ashen, airborne, embedded in concrete, in transit underground, in the bark or heartwood of a tree, in a rat's viscera, mixed into the paint of a painting, a molecule of its lucent goo? What of the metaphysics—ruminations, concepts, propositions, questions heavy with intimations—and the current communiques from lived experience as they fade from phenomenal reality? The exterior silence expands—the squirrel's silence, the ample silence of another, holding its own weight, its own beauty, which is its own meaninglessness and its own voluminous surprise.

I could easily insert some heavy-handed metaphor here, positing Time as a steed with Reality as its rider. I could insert it anywhere. I could extend it, crossing Flutter Street onto Flat Ave, crossing a paper bag with a holiday and an electric scooter with unscented laundry soap so that one week could flow into the next. Reason, in its quest for accuracy and precision would try to keep up, wielding Occam's razor to lighten its cognitive load, generating ellipses, leaving elements of reasoning behind. But Reality would quickly outdistance Reason, which we've left on foot, after all. Reason can't override mortality, in any case—I'll posit that but leave the picturing to others: the meadows, ridges, prairies, marshlands, deserts under the running steed, and the steed, and the rider, and the pursuing mind. "All of us," as George Eliot notes, "grave or light, get our thoughts entangled in metaphors and act fatally on the strength of them." Or fatedly, their determinative sense construed retrospectively and in light of events (assuming that the light isn't blinding). But on the basis of what temporal or spatial or social or subjective point of relevance is fatedness determined, what and where is the point of view on fate? What's the metaphysical effect of the matter at hand, what bears prescience in, so to speak, a nutshell? Wandering into one of the several galleries adjacent to the Library of the Twentieth Century, Leo X. Lee moves from one image to the next. One deep yellow form might be that of an angel, a presence gilded with guilt. A blue-spotted lump trailing pale gray lines might be a cephalopod, one with a dozen legs and a hundred eyes, too curious, too multidirectional, to lead anywhere. Looking back three thousand years, the classicist sums it up: "Whatever the case, the world so viewed is a pretty place, and it is filled with matter."

So okay: bare textual existence may consist solely in a name (Nellie Jane Willander, Jumi Brianna Stein, Zander Blue Dallas, etc.). But assign an idea to one or two of the names and we could have the beginning of a proper story. A set with mobilized buildings, parading pedestrians, miniaturized canines, and mumbling trees would intensify anticipation of things to come, regret for things missed. It's not what grammarians call a *proper noun,* it's not a *name* that watches the sunlight enter a room to devour its shadows and gently stir up dust. Is skepticism ever irrelevant? Irrelevant or not, skepticism is seldom directed at housework, housework requires either resignation or willingness as one sets oneself to washing dishes, vacuuming floors, sorting socks, making beds, any one of which "begets that reliance or security," as David Hume puts it, that we gain from a familiar, long-held belief. Or from—here it is, at a moment of blindness, or is it mere foolishness?—hope.

I suppose there's nothing that can't be thought about, but can thinking "correct" reality? Or justify it? If one is capable of hope—predisposed to it, say (let's credit Micah Andre Blake with that, or tease him about it), or even if one is rationally persuaded to it—it floats on a flimsy web of assumptions or in a vision of a not-yet and maybe never realizable time and place. "The soul of the apartment is the carpet"—so said Edgar Allan Poe. But no carpet can compare to foxtails in summer grassing up to the trunk of a live oak tree, and Poe's carpet is not the stage on which the drama of building and lengthily stirring a perfect risotto plays out. Perhaps what's principally at stake here is involvement—there's always something optimistic sustaining it, something proper to comedy. Night comes to the fence, having caught the damp earth scent of long carrots as Lola snaps off their tops, but this is something I can only report, since I wasn't there and there's no real story to it.

You can't just use a term like *art*, Lola says (she adjusts her glasses and pushes her hair behind her right ear), not to mention *reality* or *freedom*, and think you are referring to anything—anything (she pauses)—anything *real*. The terms are too sloppy to name proper categories. No, no, you're wrong, says Micah Andre Blake exuberantly. Lola is unlikely to feel the fun of debate when in the middle of it. Lola? Micah Andre Blake? They're not here to provide concept-fodder, let's not fall for the illusion that a name can contain all the contradictions, interactions, coordinations, disconnects, and contexts that enter into—that create—any actual life. Yeah, but names are often engaged in an encyclopedic caper, they're often attempting a compendious heist. Take Philip the Fallible, Sam Riotmaker, Lucy of Steeds, Monty Makes Flutes, Clara Symbolslinger; listen to the Teller of L'Atelier discussing *passion* with Foot-on-the-Floor.

Before there's a proposition there's a judgment, before a judgment there's an interpretation, and before an interpretation there's a feeling. I feel I have a cat on my lap or that the pasta sauce needs another pinch of red pepper flakes or that the bird suddenly visible through the window is a chestnut-backed chickadee, yes, but also that language is a better medium for metaphysics than for matter. Feelings are the flash points of encounter. Presumably with that we have something to say: life is full of indubitable things, implacable subject matter unshaken faces reproach, the sentimentality of friend selfies (the faces smiling without remorse) is inane, etc. There's no intentional cat-on-lap theme here, by the way, but each return of the cat does raise questions of understanding. Perhaps the propositional mind, the propensity for conceptualizing, is peculiarly human, or peculiar to humans' language-casting disposition. This is (isn't) a cat—and with that we make a prepropositional judgment. Actually, no cat is available for lyric apostrophizing ("O Pangur Bán," etc.): the weather's warm and the cat's not on my lap but outdoors dozing in a patch of sunlight near a sprawling tangle of nasturtiums. To quote an unusual moment in Wittgenstein: "(Light dawns gradually over the whole)"—I include it within the parentheses that bear it, what I'll call a parenthesis of feeling.

I CAN'T DETERMINE if I'm the source, the continuation, or the destination of the electronic tolling of the alarm that sounds from my "smart phone" at 7:03 a.m., the anomalous time for which I've set it, I, not as self-same as a person is said to be. Five minutes pass and then a garbage truck stops noisily under the window as if intent on forcing to completion my progress from sleep to the waking world with its false, abundant, colliding, important, preposterous narratives, which in reality are just crowded closets, or language lines only flimsily grammatical, or should we call them fuses? From the part, using inductive logic, we think we can discover the whole, and from that draw out the story in it, returning to the part (or parts)—the process never comes to an end and along the way we accumulate stuff and then feel virtuous by throwing most of it away. Farewell blue skirt, farewell colander with holes in the mesh, farewell passing cloud in the shape of a man on his back (probably dead), farewell irreparable binoculars, farewell anthology of Victorian parlor verse. I repeat: one thing interprets another; everything that happens is an interpretation, each thing that exists interprets: skyscraper, beetle, anxiety, infant at its restless guesswork. One way or another, things with their inexhaustible, generally mindless (impersonal), responsive mobility survive from one day to the next, as busy on Tuesday as on Monday or on the Monday before it, even while they're becoming different things: there's first this nematode and then that. We can do a lot of interpreting without throwing jargon at it. Pippa Sidhu Petersdot puts a dollar into the paper cup on Philip Kilmartin's lap. Pitying is an exercise of power (this is the essence of Nietzsche's case against pity), and when one's pity is rebuffed, one's power is denied. Philip Kilmartin nods his head and slips the dollar into the breast pocket of his plaid (muted brown, yellow, white, and pale green) shirt. Pippa Sidhu Petersdot smiles at Philip Kilmartin or at her power. Or she's responding to the slivers of light that flash between the leaves of the street trees along Ashen Avenue. "Thought chastens thought; so prithee judge again." The line is from "Democritus to His Little Book," one of the three poems (or four if you count the initial Latin poem and the English translation that follows it as two) with which Robert Burton prefaces *The Anatomy of Melancholy*), in which soon after he writes, "As a river runs sometimes precipitate and swift, then dull and slow; now direct, then winding; now deep, then shallow; now muddy, then clear; now broad, then narrow; doth my style flow: now serious, then light; now comical, then satirical; now more elaborate, then remiss, as the present subject required, or as at that time I was affected."

The weather's beautiful, Timmy Jay Chandra says through the slot in the bulletproof glass to Cornelia Katrina Cabanatuan as if inviting an understanding, passing along a bit of time to which inside the bank she doesn't have access. Inevitably we are back within the limits of human knowledge and reach for its concomitant virtues, the beneficial value and productive power of uncertainty and the skepticism that keeps us on our uncertain toes. It's those very limits that delude us into thinking we have unlimited freedom for interpretation, that understanding remains open as we move about, each of us marred by ideology and masked in subjectivity; it's impossible to come nakedly face-to-face with moss on a rock, oatmeal in a bowl, a dead dog. Carlotta Bobby Bausch, Tamarind

Magee, Tessa Flint Aveeno, Zander Dallas, Lola, and all the rest of us, we live in two worlds: the world of suffering and the world—not of consolation, because that would append it to the world of suffering while the world I'm positing (and want to be perceiving—or at least just feeling [if there's any *just* about it]) is independent of, though perhaps simultaneous with, that of suffering but is, instead, a world of joy, sometimes vast with tranquility and sometimes rippling or even surging with delights. Double, triple, quadruple, quintuple—multiple are the ways (as a poet of another time might put it) in which what appears seems, and no matter how a thing appears, there's no truth to the case, detection has to be a satisfaction in itself. Everything is case specific—this is what Placo Paris Wang, the February detective, is saying to Materia Tamayo-Cole, the (slightly) younger February detective. It's not murder, it's bike theft: the dude didn't lose his girlfriend, he lost his bike. Without which, says Materia Tamayo-Cole, he can't visit his girlfriend or get to his job. There's nothing like the sadness of shoes, Materia says, there's no stretch of cement that's a festival of freedom.

Perhaps we get the concept of freedom from dreams, though they're in fact epiphenomenal affairs stuffed with materials to which we're bound. There are no unbound feelings—there's nothing unbound at all. Vulgarizers have inflated what Freud called the *manifest content* of dreams with allegory, mining it for unsaid, secret thoughts, known as its *latent content*; Freud himself seemed to find it filled with lurking horrors, fears, and forbidden desires. And lies? "There is often a passage in even the most thoroughly interpreted dream which has to be left obscure [. . .]. This is the dream's navel." It's an aperture, a way back or a way out. Or it might be a doorway into sheer prevarication—this too might give us passage to what we imagine to be the kingdom of dreams, a prephenomenal world (where we have freedom before we are bound to life) or a postphenomenal world (where we are free again after we are, as they say, released from life). Life—meaningless, banal, copious: why not take it? I'm not dreaming of being released from, or even being relieved of, my own absurdity, my own sincerity.

Barely conscious of the ongoing, multiple pressures (and pleasures) of interpretation that her feet are undertaking, Floka Claire Gregory steps off the curb, crosses the street, and walks into The Chance Café, stepping aside as she enters to let a customer in a wheelchair back away from a table. We wouldn't necessarily be wrong to speculate here that metaphysics is denying reality (Floka is thinking about the ethical quandary that twists under the rubric of "white guilt," Floka's feet are attending to matters on the ground) or perhaps merely supplementing it. Humans in the epistemological world are like beasts of burden bred and schooled to understand some things and not others and to haul the baggage of what they do understand from place to place hitched to a harness strung with bells, no, in an electric car, furtive, powerful, fast. Given global interconnectivity, selective interconnectivity, changing urban demographics, extreme weather events, economic inequality, mass incarceration, homelessness, urban congestion, civic madness, monetization, "rabbit holes," electronic speed, surveillance, social media vigilantism, weaponization, what are the possibilities for an insubordinate text, a text that until this moment would have been inconceivable? Ethics, after all, are all about the ways someone responds to the objects and situations that come to her, him, or them, responding by heeding laws, rules, regulations, restrictions, constraints—with no need for totalizing frameworks. Sadness—simpler than grief or sorrow—sits in its tower overlooking the ballpark or a downtown intersection or Pug Blade Alley where it slithers between the blank back wall of a supermarket and an apartment building or a high-rise parking lot. Happiness—just as unpredictable as joy but less paralyzing—jumps out of bed, letting the down comforter fall to the floor. What, then, is the "mystical instant" of which Walter Benjamin speaks, the allegorical moment that becomes "the 'now' of contemporary actuality"? The modernity that Noor Bigelow, Jewassi Zhdanov Jones, Francesca Malaya Martin, and Lola experience can't satisfy yearnings for a Beyond: a Beyond is inconceivable, or it is an abyss of destitution, a chaos of impossibility, a horrible end. Lola and her peers live in the present struggling for the moment. There's nothing behind us—so says Jewassi Jones to Noor Bigelow; they are sitting on a low cement wall facing the library, smoking—no history. Noor shrugs; she gestures to the space behind them, the dusty ivy, the bleached litter, the slender—or call it scrawny—tree trunk (a pale, mauve-tinged brown). Nature, she says. The ground rarely refuses us; the cement is solid, even when it's broken apart and strewn about as rubble; the city hiking trails can rise to meet us or bring us down.

Zander Blue Dallas delights in his dislikes, many of which insouciantly cast themselves within his purview: oh god, he says, unnameable. My own misanthropy is more benevolent; I doubt that many feel incriminated by it, in fact, most don't feel it at all. *Bene vivit qui bene latet*: a misanthropic credo. Lola takes a tour of the city from a chair at the "maple"-stained PL-laminate conference table in the Department of City Planning and Environment map room as the city itself, like an interminable paragraph, covers more and more ground. On Flutter Street, people stand waiting for the bus—perhaps they should be counted as among the joys of life. It's not within our mandate here to focus our attention on some ultra-city, Aquo Thomas Koury says to Lola, a city beyond any that exists, a city without cement for a society that humanity can't imagine. But, says Lola, everywhere there are people, cities are in the process of accumulation.

Few speak the way they write, even when shocked, but by what?—it might be a dog dead on the curb or three naked white men in the produce aisle of the supermarket: "What peaches and what penumbras!" No matter, none of this exists except as written. For example, a woman quickly tucks herself into a shoebox, sails onto a cloud, and floats away from the urban shoreline, flat as paper, fat as a circle drawn in dark ink with a wide-nibbed calligraphy pen. Come morning back in the city some of the million manifestations of life resound in the throat call of a crow or gull or in the arrival of a gust of wind among sycamore leaves or the wheeze of a decelerating truck. As for the future: as Spinoza in the *Tractatus Theologico-Philosophicus* remarks, "The prophets were not endowed with a more perfect mind, but with a more vivid power of imagination." It's the future that holds the stuff of prophets, but the past and present are the stuff of protagonists, professors, and propagandists. Heralds arrive early and trumpet, bringing news, but, as everyone knows, heralds are seldom heroes, instead they bind the hero to the news, or, like pollsters, they bring some news and sell it, or, like "aliens," they are taken for traitors and shot. One can only dream of changing circumstances and situations or even of controlling them, silencing a messenger with soap suds or, better, ice cream or wine and stopping a storm or a massacre with yellow marbles or peach pits or perfectly poached eggs as sunny as the sun. The gap between the past, the present, and the future is never closed.

Tony van Heuvel moves the small red spark of his laser pointer across the projected image of Fra Angelico's *The Annunciation*. Where is the aesthetic point—the point at which you have the strongest experience of the painting? Don't answer; we'd have to linger in front of this painting—the real work, not this reproduction of it—before the question could be answered and probably the answers would differ, at least to some degree, so let's continue, and let's confine ourselves to the unfashionable question of beauty, not to define it—who could?—but to spot it, I mean in art, we're not talking here about pretty girls or pretty flowers. Is there any future in beauty? This is going to go right over the students' heads, Rosie Consuela Hazan thinks to herself, uncomfortable in the institutional folding chair: she looks at a group of her students seated near the front, at least they're behaving, she thinks. Say a painter—say Matisse, or Fra Angelico in *The Annunciation*, which we just looked at (images of paintings replace each other slowly on the screen), or Shitao, —or Richard Diebenkorn, —or Pierre Bonnard, —or Joan Mitchell, —or Hokusai, —say that each of them values beauty, if not *per se* then in its effects, or if not consciously—or, rather, intentionally—if they're not *trying* to paint a beautiful work but make choices—practical choices—along the way that result in one—why might they value it? I would propose—speculatively—that they would value beauty—maybe even almost everyone who values beauty does so—because it—beauty itself but also beauty in a work of art—material beauty, substantive beauty, humanly created beauty—because it imparts something good—even—or especially—if it's itself—to the future, or *a* future—for all we know there could be many—what we call the future is just a nest of present possibilities. In an urn, Rosie Consuela Hazan thinks, more restless by the minute—the phrase repeats, as if by itself, unbeautifully, this is a failure, she thinks, "restless by the minute." And—a related question—why do *we* value beauty, if we do, and if we're willing to admit it? And does it depend on our assumption—our belief or faith—that there's a future? Do we value beauty because we can share it and also because we can't—because it's "out there" and because it's "in here"? Rosie Hazan decides to teach "Ode on a Grecian Urn" on Monday to her students, forever panting—or squirming—but the Lunch Lecture hour is almost at an end—and forever young. The problem is that beauty is a trap; Tony van Heuvel has noticed the students—the kids in the room, there may be freedom in the making of beauty but there's no freedom from it once it's there and it has nothing to do with other social values like justice and equality and good health and freedom itself, vague as these all are—they belong to a different realm than that of art. And, clearly, they are much harder—maybe impossible—to create.

NOW LET'S ADD TO THE CONFUSION. One gets beset by minor irritations: the thorn at the tip of an artichoke leaf, lower back pain, recalcitrant colleagues, blockhead neighbors, cat vomit on the bed. Milly Margaret Willis opens a gap between the slats of the Venetian blinds to see what the flashing lights on the street are all about, flashing lights that are here, not there. In this case, the limits of realism are less stringent than those of reality, whose reality hilarity cuts short. Still, some of that age-old exhaustion remains, hardly the same as rhythm and pinch, it's just the usual necessity and eggs or the weaponization of phobias and fears or what have you. There are empty lists (nickel, splinter, film, cabbage, enterprise, truck, measles) and lists that are full (the drowning of cattle; a child blown up by a bomb, a body torn apart in our name). But as long as at least now and then we quote passages that others have written, others can't pin all of this on us, "for" as Aristotle is said to have said, "if it makes no visible difference whether a thing is there or not, that thing is no part of the whole."

The world is often far wittier than we realize, generating realities out of the random collision of disparate things, some going out, some going in, all going on.

Tracking time—restless, indecisive, gaping . . . tracking time backwards (backtracking or, more likely, back-projecting) is ostensibly the work of the historian, the epidemiologist, the geologist, the philologist, the evolutionary biologist, the archeologist, the quantum physicist, and the like. But the discovery of causes, if not of the nature of causation, is the real object of the work and the fact is that there is no real causative object to be found, the process is one of infinite regress and infinite return. It's on that infinite return that a rememberer depends, but much of what it carries has lost substance. Rather than past moments and events the return delivers feelings, poignant rather than punctual—but I'm speaking for myself here and who am I—really, who? Instead, let's imagine the melancholy Milly Margaret Willis, and let's assume that she's real as she remembers, memories of her childhood and youth suffusing her thoughts with the seductive pull of nostalgia, the shimmer of unsated desire. Shards of sunlight on a stucco wall, a handful of pulled field grass, a Barbie head among weeds in a vacant lot, a thin shell of ice over a patch of water in a gutter, the creak of a closing screen door—such things are the stuff of memory, not of time, and memory is remarkably inefficient. As, after all, is history.

Memories are among the things that the agile imagination plays with. Eyewitness testimonies are undependable not only because memories are weakly held or poorly received or quickly worn away or blurred by subsequent events but because the imagination is industrious. But let's not underestimate the power of those subsequent events; they are, after all, the inviting environments within which memories arise, one flowing after another or one replacing another. A new menu is posted daily at the high-end neighborhood restaurant five blocks down Ashen Avenue; new books are on display in the windows of the bookstore; something is just occurring to Pilar Piana Lye. Feed comes from food and feel comes from fool, she says authoritatively to Loretta Jon Minder. Lola has found a linguistic link and discovered a truism. And here's a thought that's new to we who are lovers of linkage: "there are not any two impressions which are perfectly inseparable [. . . ;] where-ever the imagination perceives a difference among ideas, it can easily produce a separation."

Write until what you're writing frightens you, then start writing. It's the great poet Clark Coolidge who has said that, though not in those exact words. He wasn't talking about subject matter, content; he wasn't talking about ghosts, unless they were the ghost words that shadow the words we are using even now, nor about violence or brutality, unless perhaps to semantics and words: brutal palaver, ranging beyond the floppy limits of communicative language. Certainly language can go beyond the limits of human understanding; people often don't know what they're saying or, for a few, what they say is a discovery. *More have even more typical of going round.* Or: *history chances round to knocking line.* Understanding to the wall on a motor steed pursues, back straight, hands calm, about to be thrown by a shift of meaning from expected to unexpected by the change of a single letter, say from derive to deride. Here we come to the point in practice at which imagination and understanding separate, become unhinged, as bread might from butter by mold or sharp rancidity or as women might from men by cold analysis and objectification. But let's not just assume that it's obvious that *swords* are easily separated from *violins* or *hosts* from *trifles.*

It's too warm in the sun, the temperature dry; on an evergreen boxwood in front of Omega Lounge a hummingbird flashing iridescent green, then violet, briefly perches, preens, and then darts off. Every response to sensations includes feelings; feeling, one might say, (whatever the senses register) begets feelings. Sam Luke Berlin brings a second round of drinks to the table and sets down a small bowl of pretzels; so you have a horse (he's looking at Lola), right? You've got a *what*?—Max Marie Ritter leans back in the chair as if backing away in alarm. Do animals feel guilt? Sam asks, that's my question. What do you *do* with it? Junior Farmers of the World Unite!—that definitely wasn't going to be a thing with 4-H'ers where I grew up, so barrel racing, that was a thing: dance around bellies at high speed. Lola got a feeling for the thing, I remember that: the course, the system, the pattern; at the moment of perception, there's a flash of intuition, we could call it a first feeling (coming a split second after whatever our senses feel), and ideas and adjacent emotions follow. It depends on the animal, I suppose, but horses (Lola picks a pretzel up by one of its small salted loops)—they're not carefree, that's for sure, but before what or whom would they feel guilt?

Having begun without haste and with no real intention or even sense of what might result, I continue. But I should issue an invitation, inviting you into the cluttered hour, or into the multitude of simultaneous moments (of wars, vacations, anxieties, the metamorphosing shadows of volleyball players in a park, the smell of tarp and melancholy near a sunlit tent encampment, the dirty dishes in the sink and sauces simmering on the stove, the energies and fatigues, and day by day all the rest) or into the proliferating singular world-form moments, lives strung like assorted beads on social threads, all selected by quirks of the cosmos or the rambling (or unraveling) of the imagination. Through the night, something other than remembering is taking place: multiple dreams, quickly, quickly, but each involving one or more encounters with an angry, biting animal: a warhorse. Is there sunlight, do I hear birds or trucks on the road, am I alone and imploring, afraid; what am I experiencing? I won't pretend to understand the beings ("characters") I've named or the situations I've set up—who would—we don't even understand a table, though we understand that it *is* a table. We perceive far quicker and better than we understand and we imagine even better than either, producing vivid, quick effects without any certain cause and no good explanation. Sometimes the warhorse is rearing and black, sometimes it's lunging and gray; there's no denouement.

NEW TEMPORALITIES ARRIVE or are contrived, some the by-product of new technologies or newly monetized forms of activity, some intruding on the patterns of cyclical time (in its coexisting long and short rotations) simply by virtue of circulating ideas and ideologies. We can, for example, identify electronic time (relentless), service time (lived unevenly, depending on one's role in the service), down time (vaguely conciliatory), aesthetic time (experiential and activated by an aesthetic encounter—with beauty, possibly, but also with fear or pain, etc.). And free time? How real is that—how much are we sold on appurtenances for "free time"? But perhaps time itself is nothing more than a connective tissue applied to mobility and the never-ending change, the inconstancy, of the world around us. Nothing's too stiff, too stolid, too adamantine for mobility; there's nothing that doesn't surrender the power of intelligibility. And that—right?—that's the paradox embedded in every life, both challenging and unable to challenge the meaninglessness that suffuses it.

Realizing that our life will truly end or knowing that all that's beautiful will erode or fade away, most of it sooner than later, have we already gone a long way toward losing our vitality, and is what's beautiful already beginning to dim before us? Millie's life is fictional and that's how she feels it; she has surrendered her life to the fact that it has never really existed. Floka values the world all the more in knowing it existed long before her and will continue to exist even when she doesn't. Floka wipes herself, stands, pulls up her pants, and flushes the toilet. Drawn by irrationality, held by reason, we are bits of phenomena, the substance of the phenomenal world—we are real. And as Félix Nadar remarks, "The death that mows us down at least concedes more time to things." Time is attenuated, incompatibility is moot.

Giselle Hugo Roy and Tina Madhurmita Skye are girls at sea, pirates with treasure to bury, escapees. They row out from the protected bayshore marina in a gray-green paternal dinghy, plashing to a tiny island no more than a hundred yards away, a rocky mound with low russet tanks of an oil refinery visible beyond the stink of the low tide, buoyed by a prolonged act of imagination. If you have protagonists, you have stories and with them the fact of the stories. We can't avoid them, they give us a way to concoct interpretations—to conceptualize—without appearing, even to ourselves, to do so. We link one thing to another and engage in a rowing experience. Say we row, land, row, land, row, land, etc.: the result is an epic. The story links interpretations, renders none irrelevant, but Giselle Hugo Roy says she wants to use the word scuppers; they're the holes in the deck, she says: our ship is awash to the scuppers. But there is no deck, as Tina Skye points out, as the water chuckles at the edges of the rocks where concretions of mussels wait for the rising tide. To some extent, thought always includes reasoning, but thinking takes turns and thought can veer from whatever one was reasoning about, deploying (or being deployed by) story-spinning, passion, desire. How can one align a commitment to the promise implicit in the statement "anything could happen" with the fact that possibilities, future as well as present, are, in fact, limited simply by existing in concrete contexts and the sole possibilities in the past are those of discovery and interpretation? Inside their story, Giselle Hugo Roy places a cat's-eye marble into the hole they've dug, Tina Madhurmita Skye sets a small ceramic German shepherd beside "to keep guard," and they cover the hole with dark sand and set a mottled gray rock banded with quartz over it. They are staging a moment of episodic desire fringed with details and free of ideas. Reason still links time to tomorrow, clouds to beasts, the sea to fish. But though they may not realize it, they link desire to play.

But I'm no puppeteer—I should make that clear; if anything, I'm the marionette (pleated black and turquoise harem pants, basic black hoodie, tasseled green shawl) pulled about by ideas, or I'm a figure (painted cardboard, jointed arms, neck, legs, and feet, feather quill taped onto right hand) abandoned as if I were a stiff player hung on strings. But that's okay—how else could one get anything done?—I (never naked) would always be in the way. This isn't to say I entirely lack agency—at least within limits, we all have agency: Pilar Piana Lye, Georgina Gerald Brown, Noor Bigelow (though less than she thinks), Millie Margaret Willis, Jesse Bess Holfinger, Tamarind Magee. Maybe all that I have to dangle are ideas. Well, I'm certainly nothing like Paul Valéry's Monsieur Teste, and I'm no Madame Teste, nor even La Tête (endearingly feminine in French). "[H]is shoulders were military and his step had an astonishing regularity. When he spoke he never lifted an arm or a finger; he had *killed his puppet*." The description is of Monsieur Teste as a purported friend of his saw him; emphasis that of the friend. We have to establish a better difference between orderly and disorderly forms of observation before speculative aphorisms can emerge.

Lola must have been fourteen, or maybe she was sixteen, when she told me that she dreams but is always at the edge of them, wearing earbuds. I'm more tied to reality. With earbuds? Other people, not myself. Their songs, their dreams—ersatz. Their jobs. Come words! Bring your ascenders and descenders, vowels and consonants all in a row—there's never a word without ideas. Here we are, moving like calamitous zombies or normal pedestrians or multiform jockeys on slow scooters, foot by foot through time or leaping into or out of spaces, at play in space-time, bound to the continuum we call desire without knowing what the fuck we're talking about. "By the apprehensive power we perceive the species of sensible things, present or absent, and retain these as wax doth the print of a seal." Robert Burton's trope (the sensible presents the brain with an image that's impressed into it) is a familiar one, but in this context it emphasizes a problem: desire is sensible but it's charged with feeling that doesn't know, or doesn't understand, what it feels. Bot sawdust is spread on the walkways of the time fair. Big meager hat bot, bun bot, sprad string bot, retaliation bot: bots in advance of bot time! Wait—it can't be as bad as all that! They're ideas: quick to begin.

"The rational [. . .]," says Robert Burton, it is "a pleasant, but a doubtful subject." The rationalizing imagination, if that's what Burton rightly finds suspicious, doesn't come *ex nihilo*, it's part of the whole contextual package, so to speak, which itself is an even more dubious power, though far harder to subordinate. One can't trust rationality, which is just a beige ox hauling unpacked opinion. Zander Blue Dallas says of a widely acclaimed poet, Ack, he's a writer of cynical doggerel. So much for that widely acclaimed poet and for those who praise and publish the ingratiating careerist he is; the reasoning Zander Blue Dallas flicks the rotund dude aside. Meanwhile, back in his day, Robert Burton doubted the efficacy of reason not because it's persuasive but because it is insufficiently so, it collapses under the impact of the madness and melancholy of our minds; in this, Burton's skepticism is superbly rational. Nowadays, much is at stake in poetry, and reason is among the most important since it is by reason that we gainsay it and then recover it after it has spent many years at the center of language only to end up at its edges overseeing what Foucault might include among what he calls "texts that played a part in the reality they speak of." Engagement with any work of art might involve the distraction caused by the sheer materiality involved, the material means, the aesthetic usages: facture, style, squiggles, syntactic glitches, etc. Neither *Finnegans Wake*, say, nor a film by Stan Brakhage provokes or requires a suspension of disbelief; quite the opposite: these works are made of undeniable matter; Joyce's portmanteau neologisms and polyvalent phrases are objective and etymological, the movement of color and form in Brakhage's films is paint on celluloid sliding at 18 frames per second past an illuminated bulb.

Through what do we maintain a thought process? Sense impressions and the demands they make on our attention, on our waking selves, on our judgment; on our innate will to understand what we feel as well as whatever we feel it about; on our hard-wired instinct for survival, coached by curiosity; on our competitiveness, whereby we're warring with the object or objectified world for power. We are thrown off-balance by desire, pitched forward, arms swinging and low, as if we wanted again to put knuckles to ground. We bully fields, side streets, food processors, buses, spoons, brooms, dogs, postal clerks, shoes. Infected by language, itself a medium as well as source of desire, we sound on the streets, around tables, under umbrellas, in cars, over phones, in front of a checkout clerk passing a labeled grapefruit over a scanner: wildly expensive, I say. Mmm hmm. Jody Tomás Jason lifts the grapefruit and puts it into one of the SPCA promo shopping bags I've accumulated from the organization as it tries to persuade me to contribute. I move to the end of the counter and begin to bag the rest of my groceries: two heads of garlic, a white onion, a jar of Bonne Maman orange marmalade, a chunk of Parmesan cheese, a bunch of asparagus, two 5-ounce bags of baby spinach, two bunches of scallions, two bottles of

Artesa Chardonnay, a package of arborio rice, two rock Cornish game hens. The Safeway lighting creates a sense of persistent agitation as if it were housing incarcerated groceries, imprisoned produce, convicted candy and Coke.

JUSTICE IS ACHIEVED when different narratives come into balance, achieving severe plotlessness—bliss. It achieves a happy void that can't nullify the past, it can't annihilate the future nor reverse history, but it is empty of the present, which trembles, home to inexact subjectivity. Justice exists in limbo, a suspension lingering between events. Impudent, tidy, unapproachable, splashing, retrobate, kind, unnerving, innocent, prosaic, feline, shoveling, incorrigible, loyal, tempted—do any of these do justice to the name Giselle Hugo Roy—or to Bonnie Rose Roberts, Colette Verity Black, Tina Madhurmita Skye? For the moment, violence is in abeyance. And let's be thankful for that, though it's often through violence that justice is attained in the first place, but then again sometimes justice (bliss, balance) just happens, drifting in on time, as when a drought is broken by rain, "mocking the authority of introspection." The truth is that we never exist until populated.

Poetry: be wary of that word. Is this it—is it "knocking to be let into your heart"? "I was gob-smacked!" "I almost fell out of my chair!" Be merry with the word; the clouds, fringed at sunset, are pure poetry. Lola hurries in from the street. Sorry, she says to Noor Bigelow and Freya Cyprian Slight, hi, Genji—she smiles at Genji Askari Best, whom she doesn't know well, as she takes off her denim jacket and hangs it over the back of a chair beside Micah Andre Blake. I came straight from the barn but there was traffic, and she turns around and comes over to give me a quick kiss on the cheek and say hello to Zander Blue Dallas. The rider, says Zander—of course: *that* would be the befuddling figure!

SEVEN

To live is, in itself, a value judgment.
To breathe is to judge.
ALBERT CAMUS

THE SURREPTITIOUS MECHANISM AT WORK in metaphor is a kind of bait and switch: promise one thing but provide another. But as Diogenes Laertius says, paraphrasing Pyrrho: "We must not assume that what convinces us is true." One could argue that metaphors, and similes too, have some utility—cognitive utility, I suppose, or entertainment value, or aesthetic power—or all three. Why lop off possibilities, why not operate on the principle that reality might entail anything, include anything, mean anything? It's 1 p.m. in the light of the sun at the small streetside tables in front of The Chant Café. Time: that's what keeps us close to the ground and on the move. Reggie Clara Toss is doing something dutifully and therefore somewhat involuntarily, she's doing something obligingly, she's accommodating (she hands a menu to Monty Michael Leary and Timmy Jay Chandra), but there's nothing conciliatory in her attitude. Reggie Clara Toss no longer believes in belief at all. After all the stories are told, all the homilies inscribed, it's still the case that the objects of interpretation are always temporary bodies swept along in the perpetual process of change.

Night circles a barrel at maximum speed, just missing the obstacle in the arena, framed by its post and rail fencing. Night's flurry of action is a fast event in a narrative of encounters amid the slow events of incessant mutability ongoing in broken but fecund fields of continuation, all of them framed and framing. "For us descendants—who are not historians," Tolstoy writes, "who are not carried away by the process of research and therefore can contemplate events with unobscured common sense—a countless number of causes present themselves. The deeper we go in search of causes, the more of them we find, and each cause taken singly or whole series of causes present themselves to us as equally correct in themselves, and equally false in their incapacity (without the participation of all other coinciding causes) to produce the event that took place." Among my books I come across Susan Howe's 1996 New Directions book *Frame Structures: Early Poems 1974–1979*; she claims history and historiography as the master engines of framing, the former through its course of real events and the latter through the selectivity and hence exclusion that historians wield, leaving lives and experiences expunged, disarticulated from the record: "What is it about documents that seems to require their relegation to the bedroom (a private place) as if they were bourgeois Victorian women?" Barrett Watten moves to a more conceptual term, *Frame*, for the title of his 1997 book *Frame (1971–1990)*, turning attention to manifestations of framing in practice with an opening poem which demands that imperious frames be disjointed and dismantled: "Could we have those trees cleared out of the way? / And the houses, volcanoes, empires?" These are not matters of style but of crisis, creating catastrophes of understanding and, which is the point, motivating radical interventions into the potential for a meaningful world. To use another of Watten's conceptual terms (and conceptual turns), these crises catalyze *conceptual moments*, notional breakthroughs and their ensuing creative social spaces. "How dost thou know that some entire, living, thinking thing may not be invisible and uninterpretatingly standing precisely where thou now standest [. . .]?" "This word is like a fang, that one is quenched and bleeding eye; this phrase seems to move like the claw of a crab. All of it is alive with the hideous vitality of things organized in disorganization." Freedom, justice, human understanding—these are nonnarrative frames, while violence (war, murder, brawling, injustice, confinement, etc.) erupts into narratives with more than metaphorically volcanic force. Well, I'm no less distressed now than I was months ago by the fact that neither freedom nor justice nor human understanding exist more than incompletely and briefly if at all, there's nothing playful or witty to be done with it. The frames hold strong nonetheless, generally coercive paradigms with their protocols, dogma, ideology, cultural "truths" borne by pedestrians, motorists, schoolchildren, mechanics, astrophysicists, academics, cops, office receptionists, indexers, politicians, chiropractors, realtors, gardeners, sanitation workers, chefs, carpenters, publishers, bankers, actors, philanthropists, admirals, cinematographers, etc., not to mention people who claim they are innocent of crimes and have been "framed," and once upon a time the "framers of the US Constitution." Night shies on the fairground at an empty popcorn bag blowing toward her in the breeze, Lola grabs her mane and grips with her knees at the sudden swerve, she keeps her seat.

I could say that the circle of characters and of characteristics widens, but that metaphorical circle is a depicted district—the French get it right by designating different parts of Paris as *arrondissements*—with its distinguishable neighborhoods and central commercial or administrative areas, its familiar shops, restaurants, cafés, and bars, its houses and apartment buildings, its pedestrians, cyclists, dogwalkers, families, and motorists—that metaphorical circle is a zone of local circulation that intensifies as its characters and characteristics proliferate, as they can't help but do. We live in plethoras, abundancies, superfluities, overload, reverberating immensities in which one can admirably lose one's way. "Doubts are the most intimate things about us"—Camus says that, says Jesse Malek Actos to Floka Claire Gregory and Jean-Louis Despagne, but if there were a context for winner of the "most intimate" category I'd wager on memories and the knowledge we get from them, those are the most intimate things about us. Camus had a specifically literary intelligence, a writer's occasional inner unfamiliar, something not fully under control, a "loose cannon," useless as it rolls over a cliff and crashes onto wizened gray boulders at the bottom of a deep gulley; it doesn't outlive itself as an idle antique. We experience who we are, says Floka. Jean-Louis Despagne laughs; I am an oyster in a bar overlooking a man-made urban lake with a dry martini, ça c'est *intime, complètement intime*. Well-being, Jean-Louis adds, that is the only form that freedom takes.

A spirited palomino, unwilling to plod under its flag-toting rider, tosses its head as it prances. Is the horse being forced to demonstrate patriotism or is it preparing to toss the rider off? From his booth at the arena, the hee-hawing announcer heralds the gymkhana. The interpreters attack. The apparent incompatibility of necessity and contingency (or determinateness and chance) is easily done away with: contingency (chance) is necessary, determined by the nature of the originating chaos; necessity becomes one of the available contingencies. The barrel is a bull, the barrel is a boulder, the barrel is a fence post, the barrel is a barn, the barrel is a tree or a truck parked under a tree, the barrel is not to be touched. Naked under an army jeep parked near a military base or in the belly of a tank, says the fairground clairvoyant, you'll have sex with a kind, handsome soldier named Ted as fireworks flash and sparkle.

There's always a next thought, or many; the mind, it seems, is always ready, then off and away. One idea discovers another and we are led on, gently as if by prediction or precipitously as a colt bolts after its wandering dam and grass draws rain or we stumble, trip, stagger, hesitate, sour, or give up the game altogether, missing out on developments, which are the conditions of disturbance, true, and the site of unpredictability and accident, but the *sine qua non* too for getting a *feeling* for things, a sense of how far things go. Off-brand, logo-bearing merch, thrift store sweaters and shoes, fenced "goods," flea market paintings, street market detergents, handcrafted belts, bracelets, tie-dyed t-shirts, earrings, scarves—the edgy weekend conviviality of open air markets intensifies as the curio hunters, bargain-hunting students, cops in uniform to discourage crime and undercover cops to catch it, assorted pedestrians, families and small groups of friends (Tamarind Magee, Tarue Ravi Johnson, and Antonia Alice Martin turn onto Ohlone Boulevard), and street people wander around. Freya Cyprian Slight and Fiasco Bikash McBee are at the Farmers Market on Stipple Street looking for blood orange marmalade, Freya dusts croissant crumbs from the front of her denim jacket, Fiasco points to the cheese vendor's stand with compelling interest. They buy a round of Foggy Morning, some Old Quebec cheddar, and some Manchego, which prompts them to buy some pears and some figs as they walk among the fruit stands, but not before finding the blood orange marmalade; with the addition of a locally-made salami, a carton of organic eggs from a local farm, and four bagels from a neighborhood bakery they've indulged in expensive foraging. But what can you expect, the temptations are in one place and the wherewithal present, or wherewithal meets wherewithal (the late harvest carrots and beets and potatoes are abundant and cheap). As a structure of ideas, a story is always secondary to real existence, actual lived lives, but for those to whom the story is told the reception of the story is an experience in its own right. It's about a family of rabbits, Pilar Piana Lye says, and Jeanie kept wiggling and kicking my leg. Did you (Millie Margaret Willis has her eye on the stoplight at the crosswalk) lose track of the rabbits in the story? Actually, no: they invade a new construction site and chew down all the posts. They sound more like beavers (the light has changed and they cross the street), I suppose, but I figure rabbits will do anything to protect their fields—at least that's what I said, it was part of the story. And we are more than mere voyeurs here (Pilar stops to pet a miniaturized dog; Millie thinks it far less than a dog though if pressed she'll concede that it's a canine). We don't need stage lights.

Disjuncture, interruption, displacement, even non sequiturs, these all lead, of necessity, since we can't exist as a thing without things, to novel juxtapositions, new combinations, surprising interconnections, new fabrics of desire and sense, new terrains for interpretation, and before that description and judgment. Language, lacking enclosure, continues its performance, despite the ever-changing backdrop and whatever bad education we have received. As David Hume, writing under the name Democritus Jr., observes, "We ourselves are not only the beings, that reason, but also one of the objects, concerning which we reason." Note the comma stabbing the line between beings and reason, and, in doing so, impeding the reading: it is an object to consider (it's no handhold) and then one to read right over. Subjectivity—I—a name projected from a distance of changing habits, or a set of changing habits with a name. Habits, proclivities, mores, perspectives, taste circulating through contexts under (today) a mottled sky, shadow-spotted, though on the horizon are patches of milky fog as amorphous as a spill. A thought appears, rises, flies as pebbles are thrown at a tree by kids at a construction site or coiled commas get screwed into place, but like a sentence that's only half-uttered and then left to drift in hopes that it will find the meaning, the sense, that could complete it. Back on the bulk of the ground, interpretation becomes more and more populous, fuddled, flabby (or what Robert Burton calls "flaggy"), gob-smacking, idiotic. Perhaps it's not Lola but Motley who should be deemed the interpreter: Motley the Interpreter.

One credible notion of fate roots it in the fact of irrevocability—the fact that the past can't be undone, which also means that ultimately justice is impossible, but that's another topic. That I can state "Anything could happen" and believe it is only possible because of the sheer amount and diversity of life going on in the world at any given moment—from atoms to systems, dimpled puddles to blinking galaxies, redwood rootlets to quantum gravity. How could I not? Given the abundance—the over-abundance—of existing things, how can we imagine that the future has been organized? Even the present is disorganized. If fate (whatever that term might mean) were truly to predetermine all that has happened, is happening, and will happen, then the only story to tell would be that of history. And it would be fate, not free-wheeling skepticism, that would deflate humanity's grand claims and lofty ideas. But sweeping fate only hitches us to what's been done, to story, explanation, history; it's all backstory. Lola, Noor Bigelow, Tina Madhurmita Skye, Blondie Jane Carter, Philip Kilmartin, and so forth are but intermittent instances, though perhaps now and then vivid ones; I is more so, but only because it's mouthy. Bogged in nonchalant description, we encounter milk prices gliding, pears in a dulcet basket, a fecund ambiguity produced by art precisely exercising its irrelevance; who, after all, did the work that put them on the shelves to be mentioned in a sentence? And why the dulcet basket of black and gold plastic? Well, why not, if one keeps its social secret, its chemistry? "There never was a thought that there might be, in the everyday run of things, something like a secret to raise, that the inessential might be, in a certain way, important, until the blank gaze of power came to rest on these miniscule commotions." Fate is outward-facing and ubiquitous, but its inner machinations are unintelligible, less than seamed (or more often tattered) history, less than the enigmatic waves of physics, less than the introversions of justice. No one thinks about subterranean productivity.

WE COME UPON A DRAMA of literary consciousness, with—what—nothing but stage lights to reveal it? No, music would be needed, though perhaps for its powers of manipulation and fakery, a moody tune at the turn of a thought—and yes, lights to show the turn in the face of the thinker. Sitting in a familiar place (it's differently familiar to each of the regulars, Floka thinks), for a few minutes Floka Claire Gregory is relishing the finite social and design details in the bar: no paintings—no space for them; one long wall has a glass-paned door and is lined with tall windows half-enclosed by long red curtains casting a glow over the row of tables beside them; the polished dark wood bar-counter with its four arched taps and the mirrored bottles on shelves behind it extends along the other; with a dim, short, narrow corridor to the left leading to the bathroom from which Enrico Wren Roberts is just returning as three young men come through the door, all dressed in shorts, one wearing vintage black hightops, one wearing work boots, and one in neon blue shoes with black knee high socks (the tech bros, Sam Luke Berlin says discreetely, smiling at Floka as he passes with a dustpan and broom). Enrico stops to order more drinks and chats with three of the men seated at the bar, his stance friendly, nervous, relaxed, reticent, jovial, as one of the men, in a thin black and tan jacket, sits back and laughs as an evening bird might in the waning light outside the front door, wide open in the warm air (customers have tracked a few summer leaves onto the floor where they lie beside a scrap of paper blown in by the breeze—Sam Luke Berlin with a few quick, benign [it's summer] gestures sweeps them up). Enrico nods at the overhead tv sports screen (the sound is mute, the Rolling Stones' version of "I Can't Get No Satisfaction" is playing [Floka becomes aware that her musings are attuned to the music, she wonders—not having full autonomy—about satisfaction and finite details]). Do you enter a new space with curiosity or with skepticism?, Floka asks Enrico Wren Roberts as he comes to the table with their drinks; that's out of nowhere, he says, I don't know, it would depend on the place, maybe it would just be funny. Skepticism may enjoy the comical, it may employ irony, but it isn't itself ironic, it's *sincere* in Henry James's sense of the term and later in that of Louis Zukofsky and George Oppen: sincere—connected. As Zukofsky describes it, "Writing occurs which is the detail, not mirage, of seeing, of thinking with the things as they exist, and of directing them along a line of melody. Shapes suggest themselves, and the mind senses and receives awareness." Pocked wall; mottled tent: a small buff, black, and white fluffy dog is sniffing around the legs of a bar stool, its leash loose on Connie Bobby Cleo's lap until the dog wanders off, following its nose to where a young woman sees it and lifts it onto her lap, cooing "What's your name, little peanut—Little Peanut?"

"In every other similitude of life to the theatre, the resemblance hath been always taken from the stage only. None, as I remember, have at all considered the audience at this grand drama." So says Henry Fielding in *Tom Jones*; he (Fielding? Tom Jones?) is exploring comic passions, the avidity of the eye, the arms, the aching realms between the greedy legs, in a masterpiece "containing a few common matters, with a very uncommon observation about them." It's not uncommon, of course (I'll not address you as "Dear Reader") to note that what the avid audience of life places under inspection goes on from one Monday to the next and the next, taking in merchandise, buses, the debris from an overflowing street corner trash receptacle, small ineffectual dogs dressed in plaid jackets, the stone-faced, arched, mullioned window below the sharp peak of a roof, wagging gingko leaves along Ashen Ave, a sandwich board advertising Mexican chocolates in front of a newly opened (and doomed?) shop. And now (I too am in the audience) a helicopter is passing overhead, I know just where it is, but I can't see it—it's hidden deep in the absorbent blue of the sky.

It's been said that beauty provokes forgetfulness, but it might be more apt to say it produces self-obliteration, magnifying experiences that diminish the self to something microscopic (though, certainly, still alive). Beauty has too little to do with love—it has effects but no agency, while love incites the self; it's impossible to come back to reality from beauty. Bonnie Rose Roberts and Giselle Hugo Roy are gazing at a red and glowing gold nasturtium flower that Bonnie has carefully picked from the soft stem on the vine-like tangle of tendrils on the ground at the edge of a small weedy yard (yellowing foxtails, the last vestiges of oxalis, dandelions, and a few volunteer forget-me-nots that will soon produce prickled russet burrs). Bonnie Rose Roberts pokes the spicy flower into her mouth and eats it. Bonnie Rose Roberts and Giselle Hugo Roy are too young for self-obliteration. Giselle picks another of the five-lobed flowers from the plant, uprooting a shallow stretch of it from the patch of gray dimpled soil silently holding minute perennial details by the wayside. Perhaps there's too little buoyancy in beauty.

It's no longer appropriate to present someone—a lover, a friend—with a photograph of oneself, flat, incorporeal, a chemical ember, a picture of a pictured picture, the selfie, punctually but pointlessly staged. The material object is elsewhere, an already passing and always unrepresentable thing. It wants to communicate what it can't make perceptible, but voilà: Tessa Flint Aveeno remembers—no she imagines—it with the sound of a waterfall behind her back, say, or with the touch of her tongue to the tip of a triple-scoop ice cream cone (see the tongue?) on a wharf or as her demonstration of bravissimo (would it be bravissima?) when she was at a "tequila dulce" party. The backdrops serve functions for a populated but not unalienated (she's not stupid!) subjectivity, provide proof but mainly that the geraniums in the white wooden planters on the wharf were in full bloom, or that there's a waterfall in the redwoods in July, or that bravissimo always looks dumber than it feels. How could this pseudo-participation possibly be deemed uninteresting?

It may seem that allegorizing, either as the artist or as the interpreter, keeps the focus on an allegory's content and ignores its material elements, its semantic and grammatical ellipses and additions, its lexical syncopes and inventions, its echoes and alliterations, its forms and folds, but this isn't the case: to allegorize is to recontextualize the matter at hand, to allegorize is to resituate. As Lola and Night thread the slalom poles down the center of the ring running to the finish, I lean forward and sway six poles, and they make a clean finish, with one contestant still to race. The four-rail white gate is opening, Lola is rubbing Night's neck and waiting to exit; "Lydia Bess Holfinger riding Curly," the MC announces through the crackling speaker, before the gate is fully clear Lydia Bess Holfinger gallops in, tipping her white hat to Lola and thrusting a hard jab of the toe of her left boot against Night's side. Night swings away, the MC's gasp is broadcast, that was bad, right, Micah Andre Blake asks, two fouls against that rider, Lola says she's a mean one, I think the breach was against rock solid tradition—no contestant enters the arena until the previous one has exited and obviously one doesn't kick someone else's horse. A barrel wobbles as Curly brushes it, a slalom pole does the same: as I said, two fouls—Lola wins. Combativeness isn't necessarily a sign of malevolence, says Noor, think how indivisibly emotions and states of mind carry on. This is how stories begin, incidentally present. A *mean rider*: the interpretive term gets folded in. For domestic animals, a human can function as an agent of anxiety, and if that can look like antagonism—free-floating antagonism—it's because the human has weaponized itself. What might come next—an interpolated preface by a narrator, a diverting passage depicting a conversation about a sagging fence between neighbors, a digression on money as a source of agreed-upon power but with, in fact, specious value, a passage on freedom as irrelevant to the plot, a plot? "Where 'one' lives produces a series of conceits: house, body, mind. So no matter how reduced the aspect there is a potential for clutter." Carla Harryman writes this into a speculatively narrative middle (*The Middle* being the title of her 1983 chapbook), the site of multiple, simultaneous, distinctly equal presences, and spontaneous gestures, home to reality, play, irritability, stress. Passing from one populous space to another like an exile who has crossed a border or wanders unbordered in the dusty sunlight (it's fringed with the smell of horse dung, straw, barbecue smoke) but estranged and like an amnesiac, some or all of whose past has been suddenly eclipsed, Lola walks through the weakly meandering crowd toward the barn beside the still attentive, restive Night.

As English has it, one *arrives at an understanding*, which could be epistemological (an addition to knowledge or comprehension, a gain of new methods of orientation) or it could be contractual (an agreement, a mutual obligation, a binding arrangement, a reciprocal promise—which would require reorientation). But where has one come from—what was the point of departure prior to the arrival at a binding understanding? And is the result justice, or wisdom, or the building of a coalition—say an army or cartel or corporation or entrepreneurial start-up—or a labor strike or a heist? Humans do a lot of things on the basis of their claims to so-called understanding. We need to speak, to sound the silence and to love—whatever that may be in its many potential malformations and complex contexts, with the happy confidence bolstered by misunderstanding or ignorance. We reach the hour of surrender, which we note as we note the rigid jollity of the casual techies overdrinking in the Omega Lounge. What is personal life if not our habits, the way we do things—it composes us.

"Perhaps it is this quality of rambling anecdote, of arbitrary elaboration of what seem like irrelevant details, of a constant wandering away from what would seem to be the point, that accounts for the book's relative obscurity." In fact, we have not strayed far from the question of continuation—the existence of continua, which is to say ongoing change between the two eternities, one prior to birth, the other on the far side of death. As the Sophist Alcidamas says, "By looking at something written one can view the improvement of the mind." But here it must be that I'm protecting myself or defending a work staged as something by "I." The quilted-down duvet gets thrown off during an unexpected warming of the night, a turning of the wind or of the mind. To counteract our own anxiety we dissociate, inhabiting space with a passing mind, as in a car speeding along a road with occasional farmhouses visible off to the side, home to people living lives we'll never know anything about, experiencing the melancholy tranquility of distance. Regardless, they exist in the world, the world of dreams as much as that of history. History itself—the all of what happens—is incomplete, polyform, incoherent, and always without particular focus; it's all over the place. Is Carla Harryman on Facebook? Is Fred Moten?

THINKING IS PLAY, but there should be a time and place for fun, real fun, as at a summer fair and carnival, with buskers: guitar players, a flautist wearing a sequined yellow suit, fire-eaters, tumblers, jugglers with lemons, cyclists performing tricks, people on stilts, a three-member country girl group, mimes, the burning of an effigy (that draws some cops). Among them people wander or stop to listen or wonder, children with melting cotton candy or being warned not to run with a lollipop in the mouth. I can't help but picture the opening and the final street scenes of *Children of Paradise,* Marcel Carné's masterpiece, co-written with the French poet Jacques Prévert ("Our father who are in heaven / Stay there," etc.), the women in crinolines under white dresses, men in dark rags, dandies in pin-striped suits, men with paunches wearing patterned vests and ostentatiously examining their pocket watches (some soon to be in the hands of pickpockets)—hundreds of people and carriages winding elegantly as if regal conveyances through the crowd. In today's crowd there are bikers bethroned on Harleys, Ducatis, Kawasakis, also politicians, strikers, people in wheelchairs, idle cops, tourists, families, groups of friends, street people, and Jamie Han Quick from the bakery, Cole Levy Carvalho from the taqueria, Jody Tómas Jason (still wearing a name tag: Jody, in generic script) from Safeway. There's fun to be had—let's advocate for fun! Just watching and wandering will suffice, but why not dance, we've come to the fiddlers, and the Western girl group seems to have people dancing in the plaza, everyone can get at least something right when they dance. Hands out, step tight, sway smooth, flirt. Flare it out, flame, girl! Be guyish, beguile, win a stuffed bear at a booth with a chess piece thrown into a moving pot.

In its cart, history follows us, brushing against wayside weeds along the roadside ditch, stirring up dust or splashing mud or snow or kicking up fallen leaves. No angels, we drag it glumly behind us in dirty chains. "Who can imagine free selection—which is the beautiful, terrible *whole* of art—without free difficulty?" So perhaps, like a group of children with a flower-bedecked or branch-bestrewn pony cart, we draw the past that follows us cheerfully, it is part of our caravan, our temporal caravansary. Children at play or with rubber ducks in a warm bath or taking a nap or eating applesauce or a hot dog or pizza or pasta with grated cheese are atemporal beings, untimely as well as uncanny. Now is a concrete present fact, and as such it demands. Sylvie Win Sarrault comes out of her room with her coat: Let's go to the zoo now. We can't, it's raining. I want to go *now*! It's pouring out—look! You promised we'd go after I took a nap and that's *now*! *Now* rages on the near horizon. "There always has been, for the valid work of art, a history—though mainly inviting, doubtless, but to the curious critic, for whom such things grow up and form very much in the manner of attaching young lives and characters, those conspicuous cases of happy development as to which evidence and anecdote are always in order. The development indeed must be certain to have been happy, the life sincere, the character fine: the work of art, to create or repay critical curiosity, must in short have been very 'valid' indeed."

The social body copes with and/or benefits from the material extracted from the stuff, the *hyle*, of the phenomenal world. "When I am low in iron [commodified, weaponized, capitalized, "raw" material] I dream of drinking the blood of my enemies." To what extent are memories property, one's outfit, armor, kit of habits and desires and experiences? For artists, memories are, or can be made, public property, but principally as merchandise; for anyone, privately they drift, newly assembled, appearing to the remembering alone: no treehouse impinges on the moon for you, no orange cat on a stilt, no barn owl in a canoe, nor my father on display in a storefront window which, unharmed and charming, he walks through. Like metaphors, they are dream figures, themselves transformations, and as they participate in the process of allegory they undo themselves and leave ideology as full of holes as a rural highway sign in the hills above the city shot through by bullets fired by a target-crazy local late at night. "Metaphor: an alibi for ideology," says Astrid Lorange, but metaphors can be capricious as often as they are engines or even creators of ideology or of anarchism. Delete that -ism, abolish *all* -isms, says Lola, I don't believe in -isms, the things that happen are actual, not symbolic, rocks are hard evidence of earth's intuitions.

The way we experience the things that happen can be questioned (there's the *sincerity*) and an account can be given with sensate candor so as to validate them (or us), but no true account can be given, despite whatever swift supplementary retrospects and prospects might be added in. Experiences come too heavily qualified, the longer and farther they go the more they sag. You have only to hear (again) Milly Margaret Willis's account of Pilar's filching a mango from the market to see what I mean: Pilar's good character, her love of fun—and maybe competition, she loves games, even checkers—and baseball, she's a real hitter—her sense of adventure, her occasional charming impetuousness—her spontaneity (Milly corrects herself)—her youth—she's only seven but mostly a mature seven except then, she was foolish, but that's natural, when I was her age, oh the things I would do, I even caught a bat and kept it as a pet in the basement, poor thing, Pilar's pretty dress (yellow with her dark hair) and her "snow jacket" with its puffy pockets—the real thief, in a sense, that puffy jacket, although the market invites thievery, the way it's laid out, with the mound of mangos near the front so it's closer to those automatic sliding-glass front doors than to the checkout counter, I noticed them when I was there, they're an intentional temptation, who wouldn't think of taking one—"a mango, I mean, not a checkout counter or a checker—mostly they're friendly though, like Jason who gives me a fist bump, brightens my day"—Pilar's remorse, she's no "grab and go" thief or whatever they're called, maybe "swipe and go" or "sweep and flee"?—that's why they've locked the laundry detergent behind glass, you have to get help if you want to buy any, or at least any big one, there's a button to push, it's red and looks like an emergency call button, fine thing in an emergency, at first I didn't even see it. The mind insists on defining the object of its inquiry so as to develop the logic it would use to pursue it. Milly's experience of an experience, her worry, becomes social.

"In only a single field of our civilization has the omnipotence of thoughts been retained, and that is in the field of art." So says Freud—as a scientist? Art "in the most condensed fashion and with unsurpassable vividness throws at one's head the whole trashy world: for it calls up not only the great problems of knowledge, but the real riddles of life, all the conflicts of feelings and impulses, and it confirms the awareness of our perplexity in the mysteriousness that reigns everywhere." One can't get back to reality from beauty. Reality awaits comprehensible consequence.

As Georgina Gerald Brown leaves the library she passes other pedestrians, she walks by the occupants of the blurred background, some walking in sneakers, some carrying a package with apparent purpose, some shuffling, stopping, one poking a stick into the litter and dry leaves covering a drainage grate. There's neither free justice nor just freedom in what we have in common, our being born, each singular, all uniquely living a life. What a song! You're sitting in the space I'm staring into / Anonymity—that's no affinity—to spare. As she walks back toward the school (the lunch hour she spent at the library is near its end), Georgina Gerald Brown is mapping time under foot with blank plasticity as if following a legend at the bottom of a map, the cartographic bed; impassively she continues on. A small woman on a street corner beating a small drum with a wooden stick and a leafy twig catches her attention briefly—the woman smiles, balancing the drum between her knees, playing a destiny. "Zeus," according to Homer, "is the dispenser of time, of fate to each and all." But each phrase of the drum, like an exile's song, requires assistance as it tries to nullify a hole, a void, the blink of a tragic abyss. The threat of tragedy provides just a premise, but that readily becomes a promise—the promise of necessity, at work by chance, taking its turn and carrying you into an implacable half-existence.

Pindar, in one of the fragments, says that rivalry, jealousy, and envy are the "companion of empty-minded men," but *au contraire*: when a person is beset by rivalry, jealousy, or envy his or her or their mind becomes thickly crowded by imagined persons and scenarios, in sum, by paranoia, powerlessness, and fear. Political beliefs disguise the mystical (religious) underbelly (or oversoul) of politics. There we have it: rivalry stifling camaraderie, jealousy stifling meaning, envy stiffening the air. This unhappy, jealous, envious, competing, self-abandoning person is unwilling—unable—to be penitent when the slapping sea or haggard land or unmatched sky lacks sufficient detail. Humans are just alienated from the subterranean infrastructure, it's as if it were a mythic zone, says Lola, Hades or whatever, but it's becoming a graveyard where rotting pipes ooze sewage and leak gas, and wires fizzle. Or, probably it's more accurate to say that human thinking is dissociative, people are emotionally flattened, they lack the affective energy even to sustain alienation. Lola is showing me the past and future of noon weeds in the small subsurface patches viewed as if through a porthole or camera of a deepsea submersible. But my mind can hardly comprehend, she says, the plenitude inhabiting the absence, the fecundity of the abyss, the 26,363 known species that live and thrive in the dark zone 13,000 to 20,000 feet below the ocean's surface—or maybe more. *Bene vivit qui bene latet*, I say: he who lives well hides well.

I DON'T—I can't—take the world from itself, nor do I take myself from it nor it from me. How stupid would that be! Ultimately time releases meaning, frees it, sometimes into something but also sometimes into nothing. If the latter, entropy ensues in its muddy monotony: delete dogs; delete desk lamps; delete hokey plastic Buddhas; delete the *semper virens* trees and the spatulas and private jets, hollyhocks, geysers, salamanders, green crayons, greenery itself, skyscrapers, and the sky. And then let it all begin again somehow. Out of equilibrium, chaos (yahoo!); out of chaos, some differentiated stuff but miniscule (yes!); out of stuff, some things (bingo!). But it will be a different universe, at least in its uncountable, incomprehensibly multiple details—in its leavening geometry and curls, its warp and weft, or maybe it won't have any of that, nor turtles.

Can I laugh people out of their favorite ideologies or trash ideological habits of mind—the neediness they reveal, the longing for fixed and final meaning, the quest for power? Reality continues in its indifference to us and its differences for each of us as for clapper rails, elm trees, golden orb spiders and dingo dogs and mountain gorillas and dung beetles and herring gulls and earthworms and mica schist, chalcedony, volcanoes as they spew flaming lava, and sword ferns and ladybugs and white-crowned sparrows and guppies and angler fish and blue whales and squid and horses at twilight of a hot summer day swatting their tails at flies in a field as a baby at play bats at balls on strings hung above his or her or their crib or industriously picks at the torn edge of floral wallpaper beside it. As for words, or what they say, they exist solely because we perceive them and sometimes that involves work and what we call time, its reality probably also dependent on us, for surely it's we who have changed in the twenty-first century, not time. In a temporal panic, "pressed for time" and priding ourselves on the very few hours we sleep, we reset the timing of our speedy reality. We suffer temporal grief, with worsening pain we mourn the time we have lost, the time we will lose—are losing. For Freud, melancholy (or what's termed *melancholia* in most English translations) is the pathological form of mourning. The forests lose their power to enchant, the sea is flat, the mountains no more than high, the meadows no more than grass—we don't have time for any of that; there are right and wrong ways to prune a tree, wash dishes, knit—we don't have time for any of that shit. Hurry—the pathological form of melancholy (depression): hurry! The increasing velocity with which we have to satisfy the fixed strictures of chronological time has turned us into *Monsieurs et Madames myopes*, into *personnes myopes par tout*, nose too close to "reality."

Tigers in paradise—those are among the jungle creatures that Henri Rousseau depicted, as in "Tiger in a Tropical Storm" (Rousseau's title was "Surprised!" and the surprise was to be that of the prey, he has said, somewhere off to the right of the picture, but the tiger itself can be thought to look surprised by the storm—his face grimaces, though perhaps it's only in anticipation of the leap and kill ahead). There is little if anything here that is counterfactual; though full of fictions, these add to the basis for the phenomenal reality by existing because we perceive them and thus provide the speculatively interpretive basis for conceptual reality. But we can't speak of what reality, or facts, or fictions "contain"—containment isn't their function, nor, especially, one of their possibilities. Statement (judgment) is. Tyger tyger burning bright, / In the forests of the night; / What immortal hand or eye, / Could frame thy fearful symmetry? How great the reputation of that framer remains—Blake, I mean, not God, because the poem faces itself, turns out, and turns again to face itself, "The Tyger" in its fearful symmetry. We can think of anything; there are no *impossible* landscapes of the mind.

Reggie Clara Toss puts a whole warm artichoke heart on a small mound of arugula on each of two plates, spoons a lemon-mustard vinaigrette over each, sets a trio of nasturtium flowers against one edge of each artichoke, and carries the plates to the table. Materia Tamayo-Cole and Placo Paris Wang are happy to be out together, meeting for lunch in their precinct at The Chance Café. They feel they've left violence at a distance, violence motivated by things even the violent don't know—what the media or ordinary (unviolent) people call "random violence," though there's no such thing behind gun violence, hammer violence, knife violence, verbal violence, gender violence, economic violence, newsy violence, promotional violence, injustice. Materia doesn't say any of this. The neighborhood, this part of their precinct, doesn't yet quite hate cops, it doesn't want to, a few people smile at them in The Chance Café, a kid walks around their table hoping for a glimpse of a gun (it's not hard to see one deep in the holster on Placo's hip (violence secured). The sun is breaking through the fog, the blue of the sky close to the ground; eventually it will meet the night around it, but not for seven hours or more as it moves along its way. It's not only cats that circle along the peripheries of a room. There are myriad names as yet unplaced: Monica Boca Becker; Irina May Stepanova; Matthew Mackey Howard; Quinn Ari Thorsen; James Xanthe Papadopoulos; Henry Twill; Evan Gomez-Guiterrez; Siggi Novashevskaya; Nico Found Fielding; Leslie Yi. A heavy-breathing panel truck passes the café's line of front windows like a heavy-breathing panel truck, original and simile in their own translucence, twice and the same.

There are disturbances in our microcosm, or pleasures, as of our senses, our perceptions themselves, and the phenomenal world—the world of appearances—which is our limit and our realm of seemingly unfixed, unlimited, and absurd possibility. The common world is sustained by memories, simultaneously collective and individual and notoriously undependable, so the memory-held common world perpetually lies open to interpretation. It has been said that fiction only works for women. What are the swinging chains or the creaking hinges on which our understanding turns, what are the links it swings, and what are the points of separation, moments of disconnect, which are also present participles of the slow continuum (one has to love such antinomian situations!)? To our inner life, memories may be more "real," or "truer"—more "sincere" and "valid" than the experiences we draw them from, but they are no better tested. Everything we experience—the actual impressions and information and sensations—may all be accurately lodged in the brain, but the memories that are drawn from them are selected to appear (but on what basis?), reshaped, recast into present observations and speculations and understanding of ourselves and the stuff and ongoings around us. How carefully I choose my words! All on behalf of the *this*, the *that*, the *it* I know so fitfully, so restlessly—in a chain, at a link, on a hinge, naming a fish, a wasp at the window, a postage stamp of women rowers in a five-person boat, four plying oars. Stuff is precise. Why then the occurrence of names and the "stray figure, the unattached character," the figure unattached to a name or a name without a character? Say one has sent forth a character or just uttered a name so that its arrival sets up expectations, triggering calculations: something has been added. They are stuff of a kind, complex materiality, present or potential, protean, spurious, and sufficiently prurient to reproduce. "Social relations and individual desires [. . .] become so densely opaque that reality [becomes] almost surreal in its complexity." Give something context and you'll see some changes.

I'm in an ample russet upholstered armchair again with the heavy cat on my lap—a confession without content. I'm scrutinizing the blank diary of the universe while rolling candy around with my tongue. But of course the diary of the universe is far from blank and just as music in the key of C major no longer interests me (its cheerfulness is banal and bland), so it is that I've outgrown candy. And we know that propositions stake a claim to the comprehensive rather than the case-specific, but whether proposing or not, no one can ever know the entirety of any given case. Space runs into the corner of a wall, resounds, and uncoils. So too do requiems. We aren't here—this might be a heart-bending paradox. The future isn't limitless—it's possible to bound to the past. Do we bound (or bounce) to beauty?

These are polychrome days: gray, gray-green and olive, eggshell blue, a robust cobalt. Such predicates—the light in them—are an aid to perception. Etel Adnan is right when, speaking of cities, she says, "Places act on the mind by means of their light, especially." Things take an aesthetic turn, certainly not to beauty but to sensation, to brief immediacies. It's not a palliative aesthetics: a mosquito, a single city pixel, is singing in the life of the night, spreading synonymy, obliterating the blanks, the gaps, gulfs, abysses, the ellipses. A whisper can't break it, a slap in the night misses. Disjuncture is impossible—stuff insists on mattering.

ENTER ENRICO WREN ROBERTS, more than a name, it seems: he's a two-minded optimist, maintaining ethical ambivalence while feeling—and thus being—obliged to make a decision and act on it. Enrico Wren Roberts is under no illusion that he can do whatever he wants, he assumes his will is only partially his own, call it habit, or obligation, or determinism, or even call it a kind of freedom, he says. Logic tells us about our mental processes—the process of ideas—but little of the phenomenal world of which we're a fetching part. Their respective clarities clash. From the conceptual and its phenomenal times and spaces we built into it, the multiple world insists, neither in vanity nor in vain. Some acceptance is required—skeptical, unrelaxed: to accept is not to affirm. Enrico Wren Roberts attaches his name.

Are you grieving over the unleaving of the trees? They will fall. As for the grief, it's political, social; we suffer an accumulation of losses; we can rant at the bigotry, the greed, the voluntary, willed stupidity, the passion for fascism—but what can we do but grieve and suffer the political anger that is its medium? Sorrow follows. Persistent as a hunch in the air, free-floating sorrow attaches itself where it will as thick fog leaking light swirls around trees in the park, appearing to be drawn into their desire for chill, damp, obscurity. But fog isn't a wanton sorrow drifting without tellable predictions, a pathological being self-same. The girls giggle in the foggy park, imagining a sailboat in trouble—Bonnie Rose Roberts, Colette Verity Black, Tina Madhurmita Skye, and Giselle Huge Roy—or slices of cucumber in aspic, says Colette, pushing a strand of black damp hair behind her ear; what's aspic? asks Tina, with a hint of irritation. We mourn, unable to do the work of it; inconsolable, we sorrow over the lost life process. As for the girls—they don't want to breathe less.

Reason has bounce to it, a "sprung poetics"—that's how we deal with time. Full parallels bounce out wayside speculation, but they give rise only to thinking. Lola—the name rings against the cement. She feels her proximity to the edge of the vertical shadow from which swallows fly and to which, swooping, they return as light on the bending surface is churning while the dark crocks of trees depict crows, and a raptor perched at the top of a redwood shines in the late narrow sun. See? *Tote sketch greets songy halt link bayside lilt wag weed.* As time ticks by we bound, leap, cavort to it to a reasonably unreasonable degree. We conjecture, speculate, we meditate—we will. Unreason calls out for interpretation, absence is built into the whole, melancholy into our microcosm. Oh for coffee, oh for strength, a tree, fables, blueberries, fun, oh for a dapple-gray horse. We reason to contingent particulars by virtue of impetuous will, we want to see, we're pushy, curious, and often as impious as mosquitoes in the marginal night. The extraneous exists at extremes—it's out of things except the rigors of unreason, the vagaries of will and invention. Even as strange stuff makes its appearances, meditation undoes mental mechanisms, while the skeptic maintains a participatory distance, close to the processes that escape command. In some other book there would be a sculpting poet—and stark poetry would stand away from him or her or them who is some Ilya or Camilla or Eleonora or Luc-Phillipe or Olu or Ping or all of those, why not—indeed, how not?

UNCERTAINTY IS THE NORTH STAR, the seducer, the promise, the future. The earth will exist today and tomorrow as it did yesterday, native coastal oak trees and non-native eucalyptus trees will continue to stand in the rain on the hills above the city; with virtually no uncertainty—freely even—we can say that we know things like this, we can start with them. An aesthetic flourish adds complexity and, to some degree, uncertainty, pointedly beneficial, though it may unsettle common sense (the blue of the day out of the sky, a traffic of noise crossing the bay, interpretation of Lola in a chair): in time it will be a sure sun that rises over the approaching horizon, as it's sweet ironic rain that soaks the thirsting land now. Skepticism requires refocusing, repurposing, reconnaissance, resistance, utilizing thought's "capacity to be mobilized toward different ends." The skeptic makes a return.

Notes

ONE

Epigraph: Adapted by the author from Horace, *Odes*, Book III, 1: "Simplicity," line 2.

"bargaining with what is overwhelming about the present": Lauren Berlant, *Cruel Optimism* (Durham: Duke University Press, 2011), 180.

"where all could be justified and no one is just": Robert Zaretsky, *A Life Worth Living: Albert Camus and the Quest for Meaning* (Cambridge, MA: Belknap Press of Harvard University Press, 2013), 104.

"Interpretation then mobilizes diverse modes of arrangement": See Eric Falci, *The Value of Poetry* (Cambridge, UK: Cambridge University Press), 104.

"The character we know as Lola plays the stranger": See Steven Shapiro and Simon Schaffer, *Leviathan and the Air-Pump: Hobbes, Boyle, and the Experimental Life* (Princeton: Princeton University Press, 1985, reissued 2011), 6.

"The natural result of any investigation . . .": Sextus Empiricus, *Outlines of Pyrrhonism*, trans. R. G. Bury (Lanham, MD: Prometheus Books, 1990), 15.

"Some say that a human is a plant inhabited by a ghost": See Nietzsche, "a human is a plant with a ghost," *Thus Spoke Zarathustra*, Prologue, paragraph 3.

"Nothing is more free than the imagination . . .": David Hume, *An Enquiry Concerning Human Understanding*, ed. Peter Millican (Oxford: Oxford University Press, 2007), 34.

"according to necessity," as Anaximander put it: G. S. Kirk, J. E. Raven, M. Schofield, *The Presocratic Philosophers*, 2nd ed. (Cambridge, UK: Cambridge University Press, 1983), 118.

"philosophy is but sophisticated poetry": Montaigne, "Apologies de Raimond Semond," quoted in Richard Popkin, *History of Skepticism* (Oxford: Oxford University Press, 2003), 51.

"With this, comedy lies on the brink of death": the phrase "comedy lies on the brink of death," mildly modified, is from Baudelaire, "A Heroic Death," in Charles

Baudelaire, *The Parisian Prowler* (*Spleen de Paris*), trans. Edward K. Kaplan (Athens: University of Georgia Press, 2nd ed. 1997), 65.

"This wind cannot last if each and every one of us": Albert Camus, letter to Irène Dijan, October 1940; quoted in Olivier Todd, *Albert Camus: A Life*, trans. Benjamin Ivry (New York: Carroll & Graf, 2000), 117.

"invent interpretive strategies anew with every phenomenal form . . .": Gerhard Richter, *Thought Images: Frankfurt School Writers' Reflections from Damaged Life* (Redwood City, CA: Stanford University Press, 2007), 73.

"Michelet's ambition to give memory back to everything.": Roland Barthes, *The Neutral*, trans. Rosalind E. Krauss and Denis Hollier (New York: Columbia University Press, 2005), 159.

"The thought is obscure, the syntax gasps for air.": Lucretius, *De Rerum Natura: The Latin Text of Lucretius*, ed. William Ellery Leonard and Stanley Barney Smith (Madison: University of Wisconsin Press, 2008), 275 (fn. to Book One, lines 746–52).

"One outcome of this is a sense of social alienation; another is complicity . . .": My thanks to Noah Warren for the observation; conversation, March 13, 2020.

"It needs must be that what can be spoken and thought *is* . . .": Parmenides, *On Nature*, "Prologue," paragraph 6, from John Burnet's *Early Greek Philosophy* (London: A & C Black, 1920), www.platonic-philosophy.org/files/Parmenides%20-%20Poem.pdf; emphases added.

"And all those thoughts and stories are exchanged and change . . .": See Empedocles (DK 108, in Freeman translation): "In so far as their natures have changed (during the day), so does it befall men to think changed thoughts (in their dreams)." From Kathleen Freeman, *Ancilla to the Pre-Socratic Philosophers: A Complete Translation of the Fragments in Diels, Fragmente der Vorsokratiker*, ed. Hermann Diels (Oxford : Basil Blackwell, 1952).

"It was no longer the beginning that illumined and transfigured . . .": Jean-Pierre Vernant, *The Origins of Greek Thought* (Ithaca, NY: Cornell University Press, 1982), 103.

"The command of the mind over itself is limited, as well as its command over the body": David Hume continues, "Our authority over our sentiments and passions is much weaker than that over our ideas." In Hume, *An Enquiry Concerning Human Understanding*, 50.

"Brain is considered to be a physical thing, the mind . . .": See the American Museum of Natural History exhibit "Your Thinking Brain," www.amnh.org/exhibitions/brain-the-inside-story; punctuation slightly altered.

TWO

Epigraph: Adapted from Albert Camus, *The Rebel*; trans. Anthony Bower (New York: Vintage International, 1956, reissued 1984), 8.

"a 'subterranean man' at work . . . ": Friedrich Nietzsche, *Daybreak: Thoughts on the Prejudices of Morality*, ed. Maudemarie Clark and Brian Leiter, trans. R. J. Hollingdale (Cambridge, UK: Cambridge University Press, 1997), 1.

"I have constructed my case on nothing.": Camus, *The Rebel*, 62; Camus is echoing the nihilism of Max Stirner.

"[M]an must resolve to act, in order to exist": Camus, *The Rebel*, 62.

"There's an almost ethical character to what Husserl calls . . .": See Husserl, #109, "The Neutrality Modification," in Edmund Husserl, *Ideas*, trans. W. R. Boyce Gibson (London and New York: Routledge Classics, 2012), 224–25.

"Somewhere Wordsworth remarks that Shakespeare . . .": Francis Turner Palgrave, *The Golden Treasury*, first published 1861 (Roslyn, New York: Walter J. Black, Inc./Classics Club, 1932), 237; the sonnet that Palgrave anthologizes in *The Golden Treasury* as number 30 is Shakespeare's Sonnet 60.

"There are strange flowers of reason to match . . .": Louis Aragon, *Le paysan de Paris*, as quoted in Andreas Huyssen, *Miniature Metropolis: Literature in an Age of Photography and Film* (Cambridge, MA: Harvard University Press, 2015), 213.

Wolf speaks of one's becoming "irretrievably lost, because enslaved": Christa Wolf, *Patterns of Childhood*, trans. Ursule Molinaro and Hedwig Rappolt (New York: Farrar, Straus and Giroux, 1980), 288.

"Phenomenologically, as musicians speak of themselves . . .": Lorne Falkenstein, "Hume on Temporal Experience," in ed. Ian Phillips, *The Routledge Handbook of Philosophy of Temporal Experience* (London and New York: Routledge, 2017), 46.

"[W]hen we see something, we must think . . .": Hans-Georg Gadamer, *The Relevance of the Beautiful and Other Essays*; ed. Robert Bernasconi (Cambridge, UK: Cambridge University Press, 1986), 29.

"the rebarbative spectacle of atoms jostling each other in the void.": James I. Porter, *Nietzsche and the Philology of the Future* (Redwood City, CA: Stanford University Press, 2000), 24; Porter is referring to the atomism of the Presocratic philosopher Democritus.

"a strong taste for ambivalence and contradiction" and "a sense of irreducible complexity": Porter, *Nietzsche and the Philology of the Future,* 49; Porter is commenting on the thought of the mid-nineteenth century philologist Friedrich Albert Lange, whose *History of Materialism and Critique of Its Significance in the Present* the young Nietzsche, himself a philologist at the time, read with close attention.

"that brutal, brittle crystallization of an always . . .": Fred Moten, *All That Beauty* (Seattle: Letter Machine Editions, 2019), 34.

THREE

Epigraph: Gertrude Stein, "A Birthday Book," in *Alphabets and Birthdays,* ed. and intro. Donald Gallup (New York: Books for Libraries Press, 1969, reissue of Yale University Press edition, 1957), 134.

"an image of the faithful labours of the philosophers.": See N. J. Richardson, "Homeric Professors in the Age of the Sophists" in *The Cambridge Classical Journal,* 1975 (published online February 2013), 81; Richardson is discussing interpretations of Homer by Antisthenes (ca. 446–ca. 366). In a footnote (fn 1) on the same page, Richardson speaks more generally: "The Neoplatonists took Penelope as an allegory of philosophy."

"developed a thorough critique of the trustworthiness of the senses": Kirk, Raven, and Schofield, *The Presocratic Philosophers,* 411.

"it might be a tree moving in the wind, which in the gloom . . .": Husserl, *Ideas* #103, in Edmund Husserl, *Ideas,* 217; phrasing much modified.

"do you take no heed any longer for your lives . . .": Sophocles, "Electra," in *Sophocles: Ajax, Electra, Oedipus Tyrannus,* ed. and trans. Hugh Lloyd-Jones (Cambridge, MA: Harvard University Press/Loeb Classical Library), 297.

"He is bending new curves for his verses; he is chiseling . . .": From Aristophanes,

Thesmophoriazusae [or Women at the Thesmophoria], ll. 49–57; quoted in James I. Porter, *The Origins of Aesthetic Thought in Ancient Greece: Matter, Sensation, and Experience* (Cambridge University Press, 2010), 270.

"complete distinctness of 'logical' understanding," which, however, can "pass over into vagueness.": Edmund Husserl, *Ideas* #125, , in Edmund Husserl, *Ideas.*

"intellectual promenade": Ines G. Županov, "'The Wheels of Torments': mobility and redemption in Portuguese colonial India (sixteenth century)," in *Cultural Mobility: A Manifesto*, ed. Stephen Greenblatt et al. (Cambridge, UK: Cambridge University Press, 2010), 35; the original phrase ("an intellectual promenade, with stopovers") is slightly modified here.

"successively closer approximations to the solution of a problem": An online definition of "iteration," come upon by chance, March 12, 2023.

"tangents and repetitions and intersections": T. J. Clark, *If These Apples Should Fall: Cézanne and the Present* (London and New York: Thames & Hudson, 2022), 74.

"an open future and an unrepeatable past": Hans-Georg Gadamer, *The Relevance of the Beautiful and Other Essays*, ed. Robert Bernasconi, trans. Nicholas Walker (Cambridge, UK: Cambridge University Press, 1986), 10.

"The more insight we possess into an origin the less significant . . .": Friedrich Nietzsche, *Daybreak*, ed. Maudemarie Clark and Brian Leiter, trans. R. J. Hollingdale (Cambridge, UK: Cambridge University Press, 1997), 44.

"just by adding an adverb, that was the rule . . .": See Graham Robb, "Cruising with Genius," in the *New York Review of Books*, February 26, 2009, 33–34.

"History—the purported record cum interpretation . . .": See Theodor Adorno, "On Epic Naiveté," in *Notes to Literature*, vol. 1, trans. Shierry Weber Nicholsen (New York: Columbia University Press, 1991); and James I. Porter, "'On Epic Naiveté': Adorno's Allegory of Philology," in *Pataphilology: An Irreader*, ed. Sean Gurd and Vincent W. J. von Gerven Oei (Goleta, CA: punctum books, 2018).

"Stories that are fragmented, non-linear, impressionistic . . .": Tim Edensor, "Walking in Ruins," in *Ways of Walking: Ethnography and Practice on Foot*, ed. Tim Ingold and Jo Lee Vergunst (London and New York: Routledge, 2008), 137.

"the power to wield negatives": Charles Altieri, *Modernist Poetry and the Limitations of Materialist Theory* (Albuquerque: University of New Mexico Press, 2021), 108.

"a hell of eternal interpretation": Phrase from Becca Rothfeld, "Deep Cuts," *New Yorker* (January 16, 2023), 65.

"The problem of knowing how to situate oneself in its labyrinth . . .": phrase taken (slightly altered and from an entirely different context) from Županov, "'The Wheels of Torments,'" in *Cultural Mobility*, ed. Stephen Greenblatt et al., 30.

"constitutive illusions": Porter, *Nietzsche and the Philology of the Future*, 6.

"a threshold of stone" and through "the gates of Night and Day": *Parmenides of Elea*, ed. and trans. David Gallop (Toronto: University of Toronto Press, 1991), fragments 11, 14, 1.

"a landscape," as Lytle Shaw puts it, "where humans and their dramas are not the primary concern," in Lytle Shaw, *New Grounds for Dutch Landscape* (Stockholm, Sweden: OEI Investigations, 2021), 10.

FOUR

Epigraph: Christa Wolf, *The Quest for Christa T.*, trans. Christopher Middleton (New York: Farrar, Straus and Giroux, 1970), 15.

"The day has a certain quality, gives something . . .": R. B. Onians, *The Origins of European Thought: About the Body, the Mind, the Soul, The World, Time, and Fate* (Cambridge, UK: Cambridge University Press, 1951), 412.

"shaky island of impious upheaval": The original phrase is "shaky island of tender upheaval" and appears in Arkadii Dragomoshchenko, *Chinese Sun*, trans. Evgeny Pavlov (Brooklyn: Ugly Duckling Presse, 2005).

"so absolute and terrestrial": T. J. Clark, *Heaven on Earth: Painting and the Life to Come* (London and New York: Thames & Hudson, 2018), 15.

"Combining entertainment with instruction . . .": Pat Rogers, from the introduction to James Boswell, *Life of Johnson*, ed. R. W. Chapman (Oxford, UK: Oxford University Press, 1980), xxix.

Homer, however, is a composite figure: See James I. Porter, *Homer: The Very Idea* (Chicago: University of Chicago Press, 2021).

"told of the wanderings of his soul . . .": Diogenes Laertius, *Lives of the Eminent Philosophers*, II (Books 6–10), trans. R. D. Hicks (Cambridge, MA: Harvard University Press/Loeb Classical Library, 1931), 325.

“When should one live”: Wolf, *The Quest for Christa T.*, 70.

“‘a world,’ to quote . . . Cascardi”: See Anthony J. Cascardi, *Francisco de Goya and the Art of Critique* (New York: Zone Books, 2023), 145.

“a contest between harmony and invention . . .”: When first published in 1725, the four violin concertos that constitute Vivaldi’s *The Four Seasons* were accompanied by eight other concerti; together they were titled *Il cimento dell’armonia e dell’inventione*, or “The contest between harmony and invention.”

“we are getting fucked by the text”: The wording is mine, paraphrased/appropriated from Daniel L. Selden, “Ceveat lector: Catullus and the Rhetoric of Performance,” in *Catullus*, ed. Julia Haig Gaisser (Oxford, UK: Oxford University Press, 2007), 537.

“materially opaque, interpretably complex . . .”: Barrett Watten, *Questions of Poetics: Language Writing and Consequences* (Iowa City: University of Iowa Press, 2016), 73.

“is to provide the wished-for surplus . . .”: Nicole Trigg, unpublished PhD dissertation, Department of Italian Studies, University of California, Berkeley.

“revealed that the revered new civic statue . . .”: *The Landmark Herodotus: The Histories* 2, ed. Robert B. Strassler, trans. Andrea L. Purvis (New York: Anchor Books, 2009), 172; modified here.

“The only thing that seems to be clear . . .”: Popkin, *The History of Skepticism*, 164; summarizing a criticism launched by Gassendi against Descartes.

“almost all the ancients . . .”: Cicero, “Posterior Academics,” quoted in *Early Greek Philosophy: Later Ionian and Athenian Thinkers*, vol. VI, ed. and trans. André Laks and Glenn W. Most (Cambridge, MA: Harvard University Press/Loeb Classical Library, 2016), 165.

“There is no human being . . .”: George Eliot, *Middlemarch* (New York: Penguin Classics, 2015), 440.

“The human soul is located in the imagination”: Andrew S. Curran, *Diderot and the Art of Thinking Freely* (New York: Other Press, 2019), 123.

FIVE

Epigraph: Porter, *The Origins of Aesthetic Thought in Ancient Greece*, 11.

“There are no isolated judgments!” Friedrich Nietzsche, *The Will to Power* (# 530), trans. Walter Kaufmann and R. J. Hollingdale (New York: Vintage, 1968), 287.

"it itches, it is full of fear . . .": Maria Stepanova, *In Memory of Memory*, trans. Sasha Dugdale (New York: New Directions, 2021), 261–62.

"the pleasure of embracing appearances": Charles Altieri, *Modernist Poetry and the Limitations of Materialist Theory* (Albuquerque: University of New Mexico Press, 2021), 180.

"cadaver is the other name of photography . . .": Jérôme Thélot, *Les inventions littéraires de la photographie* (Paris: Presses Universitaires de France, 2003), 59; quoted in the introduction by Eduardo Cadava for Félix Nadar, *When I Was a Photographer*, trans. Eduardo Cadava and Liana Theodoratou (Cambridge, MA: MIT Press, 2015), xxii.

"mothers are always another name for photography . . .": Eduardo Cadava, introduction to Nadar, *When I Was a Photographer*; xviii.

"There were things needing to be acknowledged . . .": Cascardi, *Francisco de Goya and the Art of Critique*, 146.

"part of the history of absence": Syd Staiti, *Seldom Approaches* (The Elephants, 2023), 151.

"The entire world entered the posthistorical phase . . .": Boris Groys, *The Total Art of Stalinism: Avant-Garde, Aesthetic Dictatorship, and Beyond*, trans. Charles Rougle (London and New York: Verso, 2011), 75.

"[W]hat once seemed to be reality . . .": Theodor Adorno, *Aesthetic Theory*, ed. Gretel Adorno and Rolf Tiedemann, trans. Robert Hullot-Kentnor (Minneapolis: University of Minnesota Press, 1997), 118; see also Maura B. Nolan, "Making the Aesthetic Turn: Adorno, the Medieval, and the Future of the Past," in *Journal of Medieval and Early Modern Studies* 34:3 (Fall 2004), where this passage is quoted and the historical break it refers to is discussed at length.

"lie apart from the route . . .": Ludwig Wittgenstein, *On Certainty* (# 88), ed. G. E. M. Anscombe and G. H. von Wright, trans. G. E. M. Anscombe and Denis Paul (New York: Harper Torchbooks, 1972), 13e.

"questions of ethics are inseparable from affect . . .": Cascardi, *Francisco de Goya and the Art of Critique*, 240.

"The source of coming-to-be for existing things . . .": as quoted in Kirk, Raven, and Schofield, *The Presocratic Philosophers*, 118; italicization of Anaximander fragment is mine.

"the prevalence of one substance . . .": Kirk, Raven, and Schofield, *The Presocratic Philosophers*, 120.

"explaining the facts of the world . . .": Carlo Rovelli, *Anaximander and the Birth of Science,* trans. Marion Lignana Rosenberg (New York: Riverhead Books, 2023), 46.

"jarring juxtapositions and miscommunication . . .": The phrases are from Anna Lowenhaupt Tsing, *The Mushroom at the End of the World: On the Possibility of Life in Capitalist Ruins* (Princeton, NJ: Princeton University Press, 2015), 217, 218.

"rags of time": See John Donne, "The Sun Rising."

"fierce, declarative and self-cancelling . . .": T. J. Clark, *If These Apples Should Fall: Cézanne and the Present*; slightly altered here.

"We use the term 'are' . . .": Sextus Empiricus, *Outlines of Pyrrhonism*; trans. R. G. Bury (Lanham, MD: Prometheus Books, 1990), 56.

"The impossible is made possible in context.": Raimund Hoghe, "Into Myself—a twig, a wall: An essay on Pina Bausch and her theatre," in *The Pina Bausch Sourcebook: The Making of Tanztheater*, ed. Royd Climenhaga (London and New York: Routledge, 2013), 63.

"If you aren't paying attention . . .": Denis Diderot, *Jacques the Fatalist and His Master*, trans. J. Robert Loy (New York: W. W. Norton, 1978), 48; the original sentence is "When you don't listen to the speaker, it's because you're thinking of nothing at all, or of something other than what is being said."

"the spider that crouches . . .": Shūson, as quoted in Makoto Ueda, *Bashō and His Interpreters: Selected Hokku with Commentary* (Redwood City, CA: Stanford University Press, 1992), 58.

"somebody whose voice everyone says . . .": quoted material from Porter, *The Origins of Aesthetic Thought in Ancient Greece*, 390.

"roaring dell, o'erwooded . . .": Samuel Taylor Coleridge, "This Lime Tree Bower My Prison," ll. 10–11.

"The person who makes our prosperity . . .": Denis Diderot, *Correspondance* (Paris: Editions de Minuit, 1966), 14.102; as quoted in Robert Zaretsky, *Catherine & Diderot: The Empress, the Philosopher, and the Fate of the Enlightenment* (Cambridge, MA: Harvard University Press, 2019), 209.

"the phantasy in which this wish is embedded.": J. Laplanche and J.-B. Pontalis, *The Language of Psychoanalysis*, 228.

SIX

Epigraph: George Eliot, *Middlemarch* (New York: Penguin Books, 2015), 306.

"'All of us,' as George Eliot notes . . .": Eliot, *Middlemarch,* 81.

"Whatever the case, the world . . .": Porter, *The Origins of Aesthetic Thought in Ancient Greece,* 159.

"begets that reliance or security,": Hume, *An Enquiry Concerning Human Understanding,* vol. VI, 3, ed. Peter Millican (London: Oxford University Press, 2007), 42.

"The soul of the apartment is the carpet": Edgar Allan Poe, "The Philosophy of Furniture," in *Manifesto: A Century of Isms,* ed. Mary Ann Caws (Lincoln: University of Nebraska Press, 2001), 500.

"(Light dawns gradually over the whole)": Wittgenstein, *On Certainty* (#141), 21e.

"Thought chastens thought; so prithee judge again.": Robert Burton, *The Anatomy of Melancholy* (New York: New York Review Books, 2001), 6.

"As a river runs sometimes precipitate and swift . . .": Burton, *The Anatomy of Melancholy,* 32.

"There is often a passage in even the most . . .": Sigmund Freud, *The Interpretation of Dreams,* in *The Standard Edition of the Complete Psychological Works of Sigmund Freud,* vol. V (London: 1953–73), 525; as quoted in J. LaPlanche and J-B Pontalis, *The Language of Psychoanalysis,* trans. Donald Nicholson-Smith (New York and London: W. W. Norton, 1973), 326.

"the 'now' of contemporary actuality": quoted in Polina Barskova, *Besieged Leningrad* (DeKalb: Northern Illinois University Press, 2017), 70, without indication of a source in Benjamin's works; this is probably from *The Arcades Project.*

"What peaches and what penumbras!": Allen Ginsberg, "A Supermarket in California," *Collected Poems 1947–1980* (New York: Harper & Row, 1984).

"The prophets were not endowed with a more perfect mind . . .": Baruch Spinoza, *Tractatus Theologico-Philosophicus,* as quoted in Popkin, *History of Skepticism* , 240; the translation is Popkin's.

"if it makes no visible difference . . .": Aristotle, *Poetics* 8.1451a 32–35, trans. Hubbell, as adapted by Porter, in James I. Porter, *The Origins of Aesthetic Thought in Ancient Greece,* 301.

"there are not any two impressions . . .": David Hume, *A Treatise of Human Nature,* Book I, 3.4, 57.

"The death that mows us down . . .": Nadar, *When I Was a Photographer,* 172.

"[H]is shoulders were military . . .": Paul Valéry, *Monsieur Teste,* Bollingen Series XLV, 6, (Princeton, NJ: Princeton University Press, 1973), 10.

"By the apprehensive power we perceive . . .": Burton, *The Anatomy of Melancholy,* 157.

"a pleasant, but a doubtful subject": Burton, *The Anatomy of Melancholy,* 162; Burton attributes the characterization to one Velcurio, also known as Johannes Bernhardi (1490–1534), a German academic.

"texts that played a part . . .": Michel Foucault, "Lives of Infamous Men," in Michel Foucault, *Power,* ed. James D. Faubion, trans. Robert Hurley and others (New York: New Press, 1967), 160.

"mocking the authority of introspection": Marianne Goldberg, "Artifice and Authenticity: Gender Scenarios in Pina Bausch's Dance Theater," in *The Pina Bausch Sourcebook,* 265.

SEVEN

Epigraph: Adapted from Albert Camus, *The Rebel,* 8.

"We must not assume that what convinces us is true": Diogenes Laertius, *Lives of Eminent Philosophers,* II, trans. R. D. Hicks (Cambridge, MA: Harvard University Press/Loeb Classical Library, 1931), 505.

"For us descendants—who are not historians": Leo Tolstoy, *War and Peace,* trans. Richard Pevear and Larissa Volokhonsky (New York: Alfred A. Knopf, 2007), 604.

"What is it about documents . . .": Susan Howe, *Frame Structures: Early Poems 1974–1979* (New York: New Directions, 1996), 18.

"Could we have those trees cleared . . .": Barrett Watten, *Frame (1971–1990)* (Los Angeles: Sun & Moon Press, 1997), 9.

"How dost thou know that some entire . . .": Herman Melville, *Moby-Dick or, The Whale* (New York: The Library of America, 1983), 1296.

"This word is like a fang . . .": Victor Hugo, *Les Misérables,* trans. Lee Fahnestock and Norman MacAfee (New York: Signet Classics, 1987), 980.

"Doubts are the most intimate things . . .": Albert Camus, *Notebooks 1942–1951*, trans. and annotations Justin O'Brien (New York: Knopf, 1965), 35.

"We ourselves are not only the beings . . .": David Hume, Introduction ("Democritus Jr. to His Readers"), *A Treatise of Human Nature*, Book I, ed. Ernest O. Mossner (New York: Penguin Classics, 1983), 43.

"There never was a thought . . .": Foucault, "Lives of Infamous Men," in *Power*, 169.

"Writing occurs which is the detail . . .": Louis Zukofsky, "An Objective," in *Prepositions: The Collected Critical Essays* (Hanover, NH: University Press of New England/Wesleyan University Press, 2000; original 1967), 12.

"In every other similitude of life to the theatre . . .": Henry Fielding, *The History of Tom Jones, a Foundling*, Book VII, chapter 1.

"containing a few common matters . . .": Fielding, *The History of Tom Jones*, title of chapter 5 of Book I.

"Where 'one' lives produces a series of conceits . . .": Carla Harryman, *The Middle* (San Francisco: Gaz, 1983), 11.

"Perhaps it is this quality of rambling anecdote . . .": Rosalind Krauss on Félix Nadar's *When I Was a Photographer*, in "Tracing Nadar," *October* 5 (Summer 1978), 29.

"By looking at something written . . .": Alcidamas, "On the Writers of Written Speeches, or, On Sophists," 32; quoted in Porter, *The Origins of Aesthetic Thought in Ancient Greece*, 338; translation by Gargin and Woodruff, slightly modified by Porter.

"Who can imagine free selection . . .": Henry James, "The Americans," in Henry James, *Literary Criticism*, ed. Leon Edel (New York: Library of America, 1984), 1061.

"There always has been, for the valid work of art . . .": James, *Literary Criticism*, 1060.

"When I am low in iron . . .": Astrid Lorange, *Raw Materials* (Berkeley, CA: Atelos, 2024), 55.

"Metaphor: an alibi for ideology": Lorange, *Raw Materials*, 63.

"In only a single field of our civilization . . .": Sigmund Freud, *Totem and Taboo*, as quoted in Matthew von Unwerth, *Freud's Requiem: Mourning, Memory, and the Invisible History of a Summer Walk* (New York: Riverhead Books, 2005), 82.

"in the most condensed fashion . . .": Freud, "The Temptation of Saint Anthony," as quoted in von Unwerth, *Freud's Requiem*, 83.

"Zeus," according to Homer, "is the dispenser . . .": Homer, *Iliad* XV, trans. R. B. Onians and quoted in Onians, *The Origins of European Thought: About the Body, the Mind, the Soul, The World, Time, and Fate* (Cambridge, UK: Cambridge University Press, 1951), 415.

"Pindar, in one of the fragments . . .": Pindar, "Fragment 212" in *Nemean Odes, Isthmian Odes, Fragments*, ed. and trans. William H. Race (Cambridge, MA: Harvard University Press/Loeb Classical Library, 2012), 420–21.

"the 26,363 known species that live": see Helen Scales, *The Brilliant Abyss: Exploring the Majestic Hidden Life of the Deep Ocean and the Looming Threat That Imperils It* (New York: Atlantic Monthly Press, 2021).

"stray figure, the unattached character": Henry James, "The Portrait of a Lady," in Henry James, *Literary Criticism*, 1072.

"Social relations and individual desires . . .": Županov, "'The Wheels of Torments'" in *Cultural Mobility*, ed. Stephen Greenblatt et al., 30.

"Places act on the mind . . .": Etel Adnan, *Of Cities & Women: Letters to Fawwaz* (Sausalito, CA: Post-Apollo Press, 1993).

Sprung poetics: Both the notion and the term are from Barrett Watten; in conversation, January 2024.

About the Author

LYN HEJINIAN (1941–2024) was a poet, translator, editor, and scholar whose literary career was long associated with Language writing. Both as a literary innovator and as a professor in the English department at the University of California–Berkeley, her creative and scholarly work was addressed to modernist, postmodern, and contemporary poetry and poetics, with a particular interest in avant-garde movements and the social practices they entail. Hejinian was the author of over twenty-five volumes of poetry and critical prose, including *Allegorical Moments* (Wesleyan University Press, 2024), *Tribunal* (2019), *Positions of the Sun* (2019), and a revised edition of *Oxota: A Short Russian Novel* (Wesleyan University Press, 2019). Also available from Wesleyan are *A Guide to "Poetics Journal": Writing in the Expanded Field, 1982–98* (2013) and *Poetics Journal Digital Archive* (e-book, 2015), both coedited with Barrett Watten. Hejinian collaborated on creations with artists in diverse media, including film, audio, visual, and textual works, most recently *The Grand Piano, Parts One–Ten* (ten volumes, co-authored with Rae Armantrout, Steve Benson, Carla Harryman, Tom Mandel, Ted Pearson, Bob Perelman, Kit Robinson, Ron Silliman, and Barrett Watten). She was also the editor of Tuumba Press; the codirector (with Travis Ortiz) of Atelos, a literary project commissioning and publishing cross-genre work by poets; and coeditor (with Jane Gregory and Claire Marie Stancek) of Nion Editions, a chapbook press.